THE
SPIRIT
OF
MEDITATION

ERICA BREALEY

THE
SPIRIT
OF
MEDITATION

ERICA BREALEY

FOREWORD BY
B.K.S. IYENGAR

McArthur & Company
Toronto

For Nick, for his love,
support and wisdom

First published in Canada in 2004 by McArthur & Company,
322 King Street West, Suite 402, Toronto, Canada, M5V 1J2

Text copyright © 2004 Erica Brealey
Design and layout © 2004 Cassell Illustrated

The moral right of Erica Brealey to be identified as the author of this
work has been asserted by her in accordance with the Copyright,
Designs and Patents Act of 1988.

National Library of Canada Cataloguing in Publication

Brealey, Erica, 1951–
      The spirit of meditation/Erica Brealey.

ISBN: 1–55278–4665

      1. Meditation. I. Title

BF637.M4B74 2004   158.1'2   C2004-902943-6

Commissioning Editor: Camilla Stoddart
Editor: Robin Douglas-Withers
Design: Shiny Design
Jacket Design: Abby Franklin
Special photography: Terry Benson
Picture research: Christine Junemann

Printed in China

Precautions:
The meditation practices and yoga positions in this book have been
designed to be a safe introduction to the subject. However, neither
the publisher nor the author can accept responsibility for any
injuries sustained during their performance. If you are pregnant, or
have any doubts about your health, consult a doctor before embark-
ing on any of these techniques.

Contents

Foreword

In *The Spirit of Meditation* Erica Brealey captures the essence of meditation and initiates the reader into the inner realm. Her book is an inspiring guide that offers insight into the many traditions of meditation promoting greater understanding of the art and offering a timeless path to gain genuine, unalloyed happiness.

Countless people around the world are turning to meditation because the materialism of the modern world has increased stress levels rather than bringing real bliss. Hence meditation is attracting people as a way to experience unbiased contentment and virtuous happiness.

Meditation creates peace of mind and is a state of being alert whilst remaining passive in word, thought and deed. Erica quotes Patanjali's definition of meditation as 'a steady continuous flow of attention directed towards the same point or region'. May I add that this continuous flow of attention should be centripetally and centrifugally extended and expanded without waxing or waning. This feeling of attentive passiveness is the beginning of meditation, when the intelligence of the head is united with the intelligence of the heart, and individual consciousness is transformed into divine consciousness. This state is beyond the frame of mind known as *amanaskatva*, and is where the union of the self with the Cosmic Self (God) takes place. The end of meditation is where one reaches the pinnacle of wisdom and experiences universality in oneself.

Aside from its spiritual dimension, meditation also leads to improved physical health and emotional stability. In my teaching experience, I have found that it is an effective antidote to stress and at the same time creates the confidence to face new challenges with calmness and fortitude. In the practice of Patanjali's yoga, these benefits occur because the eight limbs of yoga work on all of the eight constituents that make up man (the organs of action, senses of perception, the body, breath, mind, intelligence, ego and consciousness). The ultimate goal of meditation is the sublimation of the ego, which will offer lasting rewards for anyone and everyone, irrespective of beliefs and religious practices.

B.K.S. Iyengar

Preface

A recent survey found that most people who practise meditation do so for its well-documented health benefits. Regular newspaper and magazine articles report on the power of meditation to do everything from boosting the immune system and encouraging positive thinking to clearing the mind and lowering anxiety levels, to the point where meditation is often regarded first and foremost as an excellent all-round self-improvement technique. There are signs the tide is turning, however, with a major shift towards spirituality amongst all age groups. For the many who feel there must be more to life, who are spiritually hungry but not necessarily drawn to organized religion, meditation has proved an ideal solution.

Whatever the reasons for taking it up, over the years I have noticed that the people who seem to get most out of meditation, and stick with it, are not those who do it as a duty – because it is good for them, or in pursuit of fulfilment – but those who practise because they enjoy it. I believe enjoyment is fundamental to establishing a lasting relationship with meditation and in this book I hope to convey some of the pleasure and richness of meditation as well as its practical and spiritual benefits.

My own relationship with meditation began as a teenager, after a chance encounter with a garrulous young Irish guy. Donny had got the 'Knowledge' – four techniques of meditation – as a result of which he claimed to have found inner peace and meaning in life. What impressed me more was his friendliness and the easy way he took life in his stride. Donny offered to take me along to his meditation centre and, as I had little better to do, I went along. We ended up in a terraced house in North London where an Indian Mahatma ('great soul') was expounding the joys of meditation and the greatness of his guru, a thirteen-year-old boy called Guru Maharaji. I was not attracted to the idea of a guru and was beginning to drift into my own thoughts when I had a strange experience: the Mahatma's head suddenly dissolved into a ball of dazzling light. The vision faded as quickly as it had appeared, but I was transfixed. I decided to give meditation a go and, after a few weeks of persistent pleading, the Mahatma initiated me into the techniques.

The day-to-day reality of sitting to meditate was difficult to fit into a disorderly lifestyle, but I noticed that whenever I tuned into my breathing – one of the techniques I'd been shown – my senses would immediately be heightened, and whatever I was feeling or doing would become more intense. Occasionally I caught a glimpse of something more profound, which aroused my interest in philosophy and religions to see if they held any answers. But I found no certainties, only sets of beliefs.

Over the next ten years I became an avid yoga aficionado and periodically experimented with different kinds of meditation, with varying results. My attention began to be drawn back to Christianity, the religion of my upbringing. Taking to heart the verse in St Matthew that says 'Ask, and it shall be given you; seek and ye shall find; knock, and it shall be opened unto you', I knocked as hard and as sincerely as I could. 'It' opened in an unexpected way, to a page in a book I had been given listing a few mantras and how to use them in meditation. I decided to try out mantra meditation. The first mantra I chose did not gel, but the next day I picked another – *om namah shivaya*. It was a hit. Meditation came easily and over the days that followed I found myself repeating the mantra to myself at odd moments, and felt an extraordinary sense of wellbeing.

A week or so later I was flipping through a copy of *Harper's Bazaar* at a friend's house and it fell open at random. The words *om namah shivaya* leapt straight off the page. It was the mantra of the Siddha Yoga school of meditation, whose teachings had been brought to the West by Swami Muktananda. The accompanying article described the meditation 'intensives' held at their London centre, in which one's inner spiritual energy, known in this tradition as 'the kundalini', would be awakened.

I hastened to the address listed, attended an introductory programme and resolved to take part in the next intensive. There was just one problem: although the cost of the intensive was relatively modest, I was broke, and somehow it did not seem right to get any further into debt for the sake of spiritual – or any other – riches. I made a deal with myself along the lines that if this was my destiny, then the funds would appear.

They did. Over the next week money just poured in: an unexpected handout from my grandmother, a tax rebate, and so on. I even backed a winner on the Grand National – the one and only betting success of my life, before or since! My bank account was back in the black and everything was falling nicely into place. I went off bright and early for the two-day intensive, poised for kundalini awakening and enlightenment.

We were given our meditation instructions and I sat cross-legged on the floor and followed them, expecting something miraculous to happen, and pretty instantly. When nothing other than mild physical discomfort had taken place after fifteen minutes I felt disappointed and disillusioned. I leaned back against the wall and settled down to snooze through the rest of the meditation session.

No sooner did I relax and get comfortable, when a sudden surge of something like electricity went rushing up my back in the region of my spinal column through to the crown of my head, propelling me into an upright sitting position. My consciousness opened up into a vast expanse of pulsating energy, which I experienced in an incredibly sensual way, and I realized that the entire universe was nothing but pure, conscious being. Time stood still until a self-congratulatory thought crept into my consciousness – how lucky I was! – and the experience abruptly ended. But it was almost immediately followed by a whole series of unusual, if less ecstatic, experiences. These included different patterns of breathing, and physical movements such as spontaneous yoga postures and gestures. My kundalini was indeed awake and very active. Meditation took centre stage in my life for the next few years.

Little did I realize back then that my inner journey – a journey that is still far from complete – had only just begun. Enough to say that after a honeymoon period of a few months, during which I meditated intensely, sometimes several hours a day, things settled down. I began to realize that enlightenment does not happen overnight and personal transformation takes time. I also realized that, fascinating and encouraging as they can be, spectacular experiences are not necessarily a measure of spiritual progress and that many meditators – probably the majority – do not have them. Over the years, my relationship with meditation has had its ups and downs, its twists and turns, its plateau periods and even temporary separations. But meditation is an inseparable part of my life, and though my meditations are quieter and less dramatic these days, they are not any less rewarding. Like other meditators I have experienced the profoundly beneficial influence of regular meditation in many areas of my life, but I doubt I would still be doing it if it had not been both interesting and enjoyable.

In the beginning you have to make room in your life for meditation, but once it takes root, meditation itself will follow you, constantly inviting you to go deeper into the very centre of your being. I hope in this book to inspire readers with a budding interest in meditation to give it a try, and enrich the experience of those who have already made it a part of their lives.

I wish you a joyful and exciting voyage of inner discovery.

Erica Brealey

AN INTRODUCTION to MEDITATION

1

Seek felicity not in your passions but in your heart. The fountainhead of happiness is not without but within.

War and Peace, Leo Tolstoy

Meditation has been practised as a spiritual discipline within all major religions, including Christianity, for thousands of years. Yet while it became well established and widespread in the East, until quite recently it was uncommon in the West, and considered rather esoteric. Few Westerners knew what meditation really was. Even fewer practised it.

Today, thanks to a growing reputation as a panacea for the stresses and strains of twenty-first century living, meditation has shaken off its ascetic image and is considered enormously good for us. As more and more people take it up, classes and courses offering different forms of meditation – both spiritual and secular – are appearing in all but the smallest towns. Many doctors recommend meditation to their patients for the treatment of a range of medical conditions from high blood pressure to depression. Now embraced by countless people across the globe, meditation has proved not just a reliable way to keep in peak condition mentally and physically, but to lead to a greater sense of fulfilment and contentment.

Small wonder that so many people are turning to this ancient art that promises so much for so little – as little as ten or fifteen minutes a day. Yet meditation is much more than an antidote to stress or a DIY therapy for neuroses. Although most people take it up for sound practical reasons – to recharge their batteries and improve the quality of their lives – sooner or later many discover that meditation unlocks the door to the inner realm and takes us on a journey of exploration into our own hearts.

The truth shall make you free.

Acts of the Apostles, 8:32

Untitled (Winged Curve), 1966 (screenprint on paper), © Bridget Riley.

Fifty years ago few trendspotters would have predicted that meditation would become not just socially acceptable in the West, but something to aspire to. Meditation's transition from the esoteric to the mainstream is remarkable, though perhaps those whose influence helped achieve it may have intuited that the time was ripe. Swami Muktananda, one of the most prominent of the numerous Indian meditation teachers to come to the West in the 1970s, declared it his mission to create a 'meditation revolution'. Since then there has been a seismic shift in Western attitudes to this ancient art, and a genuine meditation revolution has been kindled.

The rise of meditation

Spiritual and material values now coexist and mingle freely in our Western society. Celebrities, the gurus of life in the twenty-first century, openly parade their spiritual beliefs and Gucci yoga mats, while skimpy T-shirts featuring Buddhas and Boddhisattvas deep in meditation sell for inflated prices in designer shops. Advertising and marketing chiefs, abreast of the trends, have borrowed the language as well as the images of spirituality to promote and sell everything from luxury face creams to cutting-edge rock bands.

If the doors of perception were cleansed, everything would appear to man as it is, infinite. *The Marriage of Heaven and Hell,* William Blake

It's hard to pinpoint just when the tide of meditation began to turn for coming generations of Westerners, but seeds of change were planted in the 1940s by the Beat intelligentsia, one of whom was Aldous Huxley, whose interest in mysticism led to his book *The Perennial Philosophy* (1945). A few years after its publication Huxley began to experiment with psychedelic drugs, and in his cult classic *The Doors of Perception* (1954) – named after the William Blake quote above – he described the drug mescaline as a sort of short-cut to mystical experience. Drugs have indeed been used within many mystic and religious traditions throughout time to induce altered states of consciousness – peyote in some shamanic traditions, for example, and soma, an intoxicating drink made of plant juices, in Vedic rituals – but Huxley introduced to an entire generation the concept of drugs as a route to enlightenment.

Within a few years Timothy Leary had set up an experimental drugs programme at Harvard University and was advocating drugs as a means to instant enlightenment. The hippie counterculture of the 1960s responded to his clarion call to 'turn on, tune in, drop out', the catch phrase of the day, and began to experiment. Before long, countless hippies had zapped their minds with psychedelic drugs (which were then legal), expanding their consciousness, widening their horizons and experiencing different planes of reality.

Drugs such as mescaline and acid (LSD) often triggered spectacular visions and dramatic light shows. The new consciousness was reflected in the psychedelic clothes and paraphernalia of the 1960s and 1970s, which were a kaleidoscope of bright colour – hot pinks, oranges and greens, intense turquoises and yellows – combined into complex patterns. Music was essential to the full-on hippie experience, with experimental rock acts the new idols and heavy drug consumption the norm. Tragically, some hugely talented and innovative musicians paid the ultimate price for their extravagant lifestyles and escalating drug habits. The deaths of Jimi Hendrix, prince of psychedelic music, Brian Jones of the Rolling Stones and Jim Morrison of the Doors, the group named after Aldous Huxley's book about mescaline, *The Doors of Perception*, were all directly or indirectly related to drugs.

Nevertheless, there is little doubt that the drugs culture and psychedelia paved the way for a rebirth of spiritual values. Glimpses of mystical states are not unusual during mescaline and acid trips, as normal perceptions of space and time are broken down and the barriers between us and everything around us dissolve. Unfortunately, bad trips and flashbacks were occupational hazards on the psychedelic road to enlightenment and the more serious dangers of drugs, as well as their limitations as a means to lasting illumination, were becoming all too apparent. The quest for the meaning of life, and more enduring methods of enlightenment, turned eastwards. Young people in their droves began packing their bags and setting off on the hippie trail – to India, Nepal, Kashmir – in search of a new way of life, spiritual wisdom and self-discovery.

A pyschedelic bagpipe party of 1969, at the height of the hippie era,
when the different states of consciousness experienced through drugs
began to lead to a search for deeper inner meaning and peace as
embodied in the meditative traditions of the East.

Many discovered meditation during their travels to the East and shared the discovery with others when they came home. Others stayed on and explored alternative lifestyles – within the hippie colonies on the beaches of Goa, in the ashrams of Rishikesh, and much besides – that promised freedom, unlimited supplies of hashish, spiritual connection and adventure. Meanwhile, back home, the Beatles caught the mood of the times and, led by George Harrison, demonstrated India's influence on them creatively and spiritually in their seminal album *Sgt. Peppers Lonely Hearts Club Band*. The soundtrack of Harrison's 'Within you Without You' features the sitar, tabla and other Indian instruments, while the words convey his burgeoning interest in meditation:

Try to realise it's all within yourself
no-one else can make you change...
...When you've seen beyond yourself –
then you may find, peace of mind, is waiting there
And the time will come when you see we're all one,
and life flows on within you and without you.

Within you Without you, George Harrison

Paul McCartney and George Harrison of the Beatles, with Paul's girlfriend, Jane Asher, at the feet of the Maharishi Mahesh Yogi in 1968.

Anyone who can think can meditate.

Maharishi Mahesh Yogi

The traffic between the East and the West was not all one way. As fast as the hippies were going East, gurus and spiritual teachers from the East were travelling West, bringing their own brands of spirituality in response to the Western thirst for Eastern wisdom. One of these was the Maharishi Mahesh Yogi, who first travelled from India to the West in the late 1950s. His mission to spread his technique of Transcendental Meditation® (TM®) throughout the world met with some success in the early 1960s, but really took off in 1967 when the Beatles met him on tour in the UK and briefly became his disciples. They publicly renounced drugs, announcing that they no longer needed them now they had discovered meditation, and followed him to India. Disillusionment with the Maharishi followed, but meditation became a way of life for Harrison, and TM® remains one of the most widely practised and most intensively researched forms of meditation, with a vast body of research backing up its claims to reduce stress and promote health and creativity through transcendental states of consciousness. Like most forms of meditation, the ultimate goal of TM® is self-realization, or 'cosmic consciousness' as the Maharishi calls it.

The masters of cosmic consciousness came not just from India, but from Tibet, whose religious leaders had been driven from their homeland by the Chinese invasion, from Japan and elsewhere. Spiritual philosophies and practices like yoga, Zen and other forms of Buddhism and Hinduism were uprooted and exported to the West, and found an appreciative audience.

In the intervening years since then, Eastern forms of wisdom have evolved to suit the ways of their new devotees and have adapted to their new environment. They have also proven subject to the same fads and fashions as everything else in the West. Yoga in particular has enjoyed tremendous popularity in the last decade. These days, everyone knows what yoga is, or at least they think they do. It's getting to the point when the yoga cognoscenti of the West can name more kinds of hatha yoga (the yoga of physical action) than they can types of cheese. For starters there's the super-trendy and for-the-super-fit-only Bikram yoga, in which highly demanding poses are practised in sauna-like conditions; then there's the fast-paced, athletic and often ultra-competitive ashtanga; purists are more likely to settle for the slower, yet still demanding, highly structured and precise style of Iyengar yoga; those who like a more serene approach often find it in Sivananda yoga. Yoga studios and classes have sprung up on virtually every street corner in fashionable areas and much discussion goes on in yoga circles about the pros and cons of different styles and teachers. The fact that many hatha yoga poses originated as positions for sitting still over long periods in meditation is often forgotten; in its Western setting hatha yoga has become separated from its role as part of an overall system of spiritual purification. The traditional asceticism once associated with yoga holds little charm for the average Western yogi, who is much more likely to embrace material values. The fashion industry has not been slow to latch on to

How does a person awaken and sustain the deepest creative flow within him – or herself without the support of someone who has experienced the process already? Swami Chetananda

this. Yoga kit – the clothing, the mats, the matching designer mat covers and bags, the blocks and the belts – is good business. Yoga and meditation teachers of an entrepreneurial bent have got ahead of the game and learned to play the publicity machine, and many gurus have become celebrities – even brands – in their own right.

Yoga's fashionableness, combined with the fact that many Westerners take it up for its effect on the body beautiful rather than on the mind, worries some die-hards, who fear that the inner teachings of yoga are being lost. Other serious practitioners celebrate its popularity, however, reasoning that any motive for practising yoga is better than none. Sooner or later, as yoga works its subtle magic, all practitioners discover the deeper purpose of the postures, which is to draw the attention inwards. Whatever the reasons for taking it up – and all are positive – yoga is best practised by connecting the postures with breathing. Aligning the body with the breath, fusing movement and breathing, we begin to find the still point at the centre of each posture and experience meditative states. Yoga may be following its own evolutionary course, in parallel with the evolution of its practitioners, but whatever its outer trappings, the subtle effects of yoga on the psyche are undiminished.

Yoga and meditation have arrived in the West and look set to stay. The last half century has revolutionized the way we think about meditation and seen it grow from a tiny speck on the horizon of our collective consciousness to emerge into the full glare of public awareness. Although teachings may on occasion become diluted, we are nevertheless fortunate to live at a time when these hitherto hidden teachings are so easily (if not freely!) available, and can be incorporated into our existing lifestyles without requiring us to abandon worldly life.

Ideally we will find a genuine teacher, or teachers, who can guide us along the inner path, to kick-start the process of meditation and deepen it. It is said that when the student is ready the teacher appears, a meeting often characterized by a sense of recognition, or destiny. Whether or not that is your experience – and whatever your heart tells you – it pays to observe carefully and avoid hasty decisions. Ultimately, the real teacher is the inner guide, the wisdom that lies at the heart of each one of us. The outer teacher points the way to the inner, and introduces us.

There can be no substitute for a living flesh-and-blood teacher, but this book aims to capture the spirit of meditation and to inform and inspire all who seek to understand more about it and, hopefully, experiment with it.

Look within, and behold how the moonbeams of that
Hidden One shine in you…There the wise man is speechless;
for this truth may never be found in Vedas or in books.'

Kabir

What is meditation?

At the still point of the turning world. Neither flesh nor fleshless;

Neither from nor towards; at the still point, there the dance is,

But neither arrest nor movement. And do not call it fixity,

Where past and future are gathered. Neither movement from nor towards,

Neither ascent nor decline. Except for the point, the still point,

There would be no dance, and there is only the dance.

I can only say, there we have been: but I cannot say where.

And I cannot say, how long, for that is to place it in time.

Burnt Norton, T.S. Eliot

This self cannot be attained by instruction, nor by intellectual power, nor even through much hearing. He is to be attained only by the one whom the (self) chooses. To such a one the self reveals his own nature. *Katha Upanishad*

Meditation is a state

'To explain a work of art is to bark up the wrong tree,' as Picasso once said. The same could be said of meditation. It is the subjective experience that is the starting point, not the facts and 'isms' associated with it. Meditation is a state you slip into, a bit like when you drift into sleep and, just as sleep can be anything from a light nap to dream-filled deep slumber, so meditation can be experienced in many ways and on many levels, with more or less intensity. By its very nature meditation eludes definition, but it could be described as a state of higher consciousness in which normal thought processes are transcended.

An expansive awareness and spaciousness arise in meditation and a deep inner calm. Timelessness and a consciousness of the 'is-ness' of the moment are also common features. As the Tibetan Buddhist meditation teacher Chogyam Trungpa puts it, meditation is being 'fully in the nowness of the moment'. Entering into deep meditation for the first time is often accompanied by a sense of recognition: the feeling that you have been there before, that you are rediscovering what you always were and have always known – your true nature. So meditation is also described as the original state or simply as coming home.

Meditation is a practice

The trouble with descriptions and definitions of meditation is that, unless you can identify with them, they don't actually mean very much. Meditation is a state of being rather than doing, but paradoxically to experience it you have to try 'doing' it (a practice meditation follows on page 32).

A few people – usually advanced meditators – find their minds turn inwards with ease and settle quite naturally into stillness, but the vast majority of us need to employ techniques to help quieten our minds and reach meditation. By sitting in a meditation position and trying to focus our attention, with or without the help of any particular technique, and by making an effort to let our thoughts be without engaging with them, we are practising meditation. Even if nothing seems to be happening, even if instead of quietening down our minds seem to be going into overdrive, inner work is going on. Patient persistence will sooner or later be rewarded with deep meditation.

In fact, many people who do not practise formal meditation occasionally experience fleeting glimpses of meditative states – spontaneously occurring 'highs'. These usually arise when they are very relaxed, often in a natural environment, or else when they are totally absorbed in something to the exclusion of all else. The power of music, for example, to induce transcendent states is legendary. These principles of relaxation and absorption form the basis for the many meditation techniques that involve concentrating the mind on a single thought or object. This can be almost anything: the tip of your nose, a rose petal, the fragrance of jasmine, the twang of a guitar string, the feeling of love or the image of a favourite deity. The breath or a mantra, often in combination, are frequently employed in meditation because they are universal methods that work for most people. The Indian sage Patanjali, who systematized and classified yoga, defines meditation as 'a steady, continuous flow of attention directed towards the same point or region'. When our minds are completely merged with the object of our attention, meditation arises spontaneously.

But this usually takes practice. When we first begin to meditate and turn our attention inwards it can be a shock to realize just how unruly our minds are. Most people are unable to focus for more than a moment or two before they find themselves miles away, carried off on trains of thought and mental chatter – idly thinking about work, the people in their lives, going over old scenarios or envisioning new ones, having imaginary conversations, making plans. A common, but misguided, response to this is to try to forcefully subdue the mind. This is soon followed by the discovery that it does not work. The mind is like a monkey in that it has all manner of means to distract. A well-known story tells how a famous sitar player, who was having difficulty with meditation, appealed to the Buddha for help. 'You are a great musician,' the Buddha replied. 'How do you tune your instrument?' The sitar player replied that to produce the most melodious sound the strings should be neither too tight, nor too loose. 'Likewise,' said the Buddha, 'the mind should neither be too tightly controlled, nor should it be allowed to wander.' The art of meditation lies in finding this delicate balance: letting the mind be without allowing it to run riot. Meditation is the practice of gently bringing your attention back to your chosen focus or technique whenever you notice it has wandered.

It is important to realize, however, that techniques of meditation are means not ends, and should not be made into icons. The point of meditation practice is not to become preoccupied with a particular thought or object, but to enter into meditation. The various techniques are simply different pathways into the inner dimension that are useful so long as you need them.

Meditation is a process

Through regular practice the layers of thought and emotion that block our view of the inner landscape are cleared away and we begin to get glimpses of a different reality. We may have all kinds of meditation experiences – lights, visions, intuitions, feelings of love or bliss, an almost tangible sensation of energy flowing through the body, often in the region of the spine, altered patterns of breathing or spontaneous physical movements and momentary flashes of an enlightened state. These are signs of progress, though they can distract and hold us back if we get hooked on them.

Dramatic as they can be, meditation is not just about having a few experiences: it is about inner transformation.

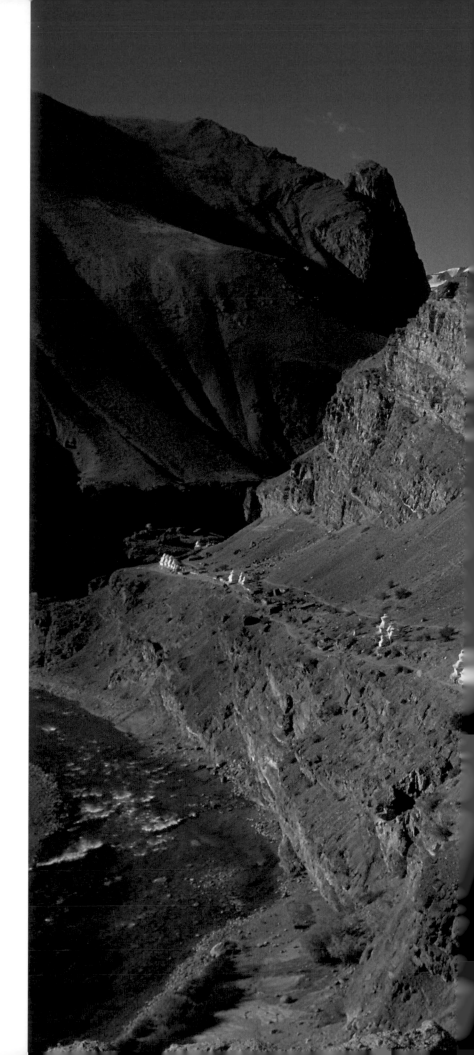

Regularly dipping into the still waters of the inner space gradually permeates our everyday lives. We are more able to remain calm and centred and bounce back more quickly from setbacks. On a deeper level, as we shall see later on in 'The Benefits of Meditation' (pages 35–44), we enter into a new relationship with our own consciousness, gradually uncovering aspects of ourselves that may have been hidden or blocked off. The invisible chains of subconscious thought that imprison us, driving us along the same well-worn tracks to repeat the same old behaviour patterns, like a caged tiger pacing up and down the narrow path it has created for itself, fade under the spotlight of consciousness. Meditation is a process of inner purification, of coming unstuck from our ruts. As the landscape of the inner territory alters, so does the platform upon which we live our lives.

A lama meditates in the mountains of India.

Where is the wisdom we have lost in knowledge?
Where is the knowledge we have lost in information?

Choruses from 'The Rock', T.S. Eliot

17th century Jain votive painting from Rajasthan, used as an aid to meditation.

No amount of reading and learning can teach us meditation, no matter how deep our intellect and extensive our knowledge. This is true whether we take up meditation to improve our health and relax a little, for personal growth and to find peace of mind, or for its spiritual dimension. Teachers of meditation and yoga have always stressed the importance of practice over theory and the higher our sights are set, the

Practice vs theory

more this applies. Many mystics have rejected not only the holy scriptures of their various religious traditions as a means of discovering eternal truths, but the entire apparatus of religion and piety.

To get a taste of meditation, find a quiet spot where you will not be disturbed and spend a few minutes becoming fully present in the 'nowness' of the moment, using the exercise on the page that follows. Resting your attention in the breath helps you stay present and aware.

It goes almost without saying that the ability to enter into deep meditation takes practice, though beginner's luck is by no means uncommon. Approaching meditation with enthusiasm can bring rapid and dynamic results. Just as you get more out of art if you really look at it and connect with it than if you visit an art gallery as a kind of obligation, so you will enjoy and receive more from meditation if you practise with enjoyment and interest, and not as another task to tick off because it is 'good' for you.

Lay aside expectations – they only impose limitations – and be as open as you can, accepting whatever happens as your individual meditative experience. Avoid judgement – there is no such thing as a right or wrong meditation. Just relax into the experience and enjoy it.

A practice meditation

Read the meditation instructions through completely once or twice before you begin. You may find it helpful to record them, but be sure to leave plenty of space between each instruction. You may also find it helpful to set a timer for fifteen minutes, or longer if you are an experienced meditator.

Sit comfortably in any cross-legged position, or on a chair if you prefer with your legs uncrossed and your feet flat on the floor. Hold your back, head and neck erect yet relaxed. Tuck in your chin and place your hands in your lap or on your thighs. With the weight of your body centred over your sitting bones, feel these bones pressing down and your spine elongating, as though an invisible string were lifting you from the base of your spine through the crown of your head towards the ceiling. Placing a cushion beneath you to raise your hips will help keep your back in an upright position, increasing the flow of meditative energy circulating through the body.

Now close your eyes and in your own time bring your awareness to your body. Notice how your body feels. Where is your centre of gravity? Feel the contact between your body and the floor or the chair. Observe any sensations of heat or cold. How do your clothes feel against your body – are they tight and restricting, or light and comfortable?

Scan your body for any pockets of tension and relax with the help of your breath, breathing in energy, breathing out tension. Notice the currents of energy swirling through your body as you breathe in and out.

Keep aware of your breathing without disturbing its natural rhythm, noting the different sensations as the breath enters your body and as it leaves. Stay with the feeling of the breath. Imagine you are merging into it.

Remaining centred in your breathing, notice any thoughts and images that arise and let them drift past, like clouds in the sky, without getting caught up in them. Become aware of underlying feelings and emotions without judgement or comment. If you find your attention has wandered, gently bring it back to the breath without trying to shut out thoughts or fantasies. Just keep returning to the breath, dissolving into the breath.

At the end of the session open your eyes slowly and sit quietly for a few moments.

Meditation is the basis of all inner work.

Swami Durgananda

Before research studies confirmed its beneficial effects on physical and mental health, meditation was invariably practised as part of a spiritual journey: a search for eternal truths, lasting happiness and peace of mind. Without involving any beliefs or value systems, meditation promises answers to the age-old questions of spiritual travel:

Who am I? Why am I here? Where am I going?

The benefits of meditation

Now that word has spread about its astonishing side-effects – improved health, stress relief, decreased levels of anxiety, anger and depression, increased energy, greater creativity, self-confidence and self-esteem, not to mention the anti-ageing benefits – the reasons people take up meditation are diverse. Surveys indicate that most of us practise it to relax, de-stress and boost our health, though in the course of regular practice our aims often undergo a subtle transformation, becoming broader and often more spiritually oriented.

Whatever your intentions may be – and any reason for meditating is a good one – it is important to clarify them and set goals, as with any other endeavour. If you meditate to relax a little, that is probably what you will get out of it. On the other hand, if you are searching for enlightenment and the inner transformation implicit in the journey towards it, then your experience of meditation is likely to be very different. Setting goals and a clear intent energize the whole process of meditation and help you meditate more effectively.

A paradox of meditation is that although we do it with a view to achieving certain goals, in actual practice striving is counterproductive. Important as it is to be clear about what we want from meditation, when we actually sit to meditate, goals should be laid aside and we should simply relax into the experience without expectation. Expectations impose limitations on meditative experience and take us away from our goals rather than move us closer towards them.

Meditation has been shown to be able to play a part in relieving a host of mind-made illnesses, from anxiety to heart disease.   Dr Malcolm Carruthers

Therapeutic benefits

The health benefits of meditation are well-known and so wide-ranging it is beyond the scope of this book to itemize them or go into detail, but major benefits include:

● **Boosting the immune system**

Recent research has found that meditation can help us fight off illness by boosting the immune system. Volunteers who meditated for eight weeks proved to have higher levels of antibodies in their bloodstreams than those who did not, suggesting that the state of relaxed awareness associated with meditation helps the body to repair itself.

● **Relief from stress and stress-related conditions**

Meditation has been dubbed 'the relaxation response' because it counteracts the 'fight–flight' response, stemming the flow of hormones released into our bodies when we feel threatened or stressed. Stress is a vital survival mechanism, the body's natural physiological reaction to a challenging situation that enables us to make quick decisions and take effective action. It is only when pressure is unabated and we are continuously stressed out that it becomes damaging. Prolonged stress compromises the immune system and places a huge strain on the cardiovascular system. The list of illnesses in which it is implicated is long and doubtless familiar, and includes high blood pressure, heart disease, some forms of cancer and some infectious diseases, such as the common cold. Stress is also a major factor in migraine and insomnia, plays a role in drug and alcohol abuse, and is associated with emotional and psychological problems such as anxiety, panic attacks and depression.

Meditation is a highly effective antidote to stress, literally switching off the flow of stress hormones and reversing the biochemical changes in our bodies that they trigger. By stopping stress from building up, meditation provides relief from the damaging effects of chronic stress and stress-related conditions, and restores the body's natural balance.

● **Slowing down the ageing process**

Nothing known to man can guarantee eternal youth or ageless ageing, but insofar as anything can be called the elixir of life, it has to be meditation. Not only does it relieve stress, one of the major factors in premature ageing, but in a test measuring blood pressure, hearing and eyesight, the average performance of short-term meditators was found to be equivalent to that of people five years younger, while longer-term meditators (five years or more) performed as though they were twelve years younger than their chronological age. On physical appearance meditation also scores highly. Dipping into the still waters of our innermost being imparts a radiance not even the most advanced face cream could improve on and as stress dissolves, frown lines smooth out and the complexion looks visibly refreshed and more youthful.

● **Increasing creative abilities and improving performance**

Related to meditation's anti-ageing effects are an overall

improvement in all aspects of mental performance: faster reaction times, clearer thinking, increased creativity, intelligence and productiveness, and a greater ability to focus. This has obvious implications both personally and professionally, leading to greater success in the workplace and a more fulfilling life.

● **Emotional wellbeing**

Meditators report increased self-awareness, self-confidence and self-esteem, feeling happier and more balanced emotionally. Relationships also improve as we become more aware and able to diffuse tensions before they reach flash-point.

As mentioned above, the goals you set for yourself in meditation affect your experience of it. The higher your goals, the more intense the process of purification as the inner spring-cleaning gets underway. Similarly, difficult relationships can intensify before they move on and improve. The fact that you meditate does not mean your fraught relationship with your wayward teenage daughter will be transformed overnight or that her behaviour will change. But it does encourage better communication and helps you to accept people for who and what they are as opposed to who and what you want them to be.

The rose represents the mystical centre, or heart, and stands for perfection and completion.

Letting go

A Zen story tells of a master and his young disciple who were travelling together by foot, following a path that crossed a shallow river. It had been raining heavily and at the river bank they encountered a beautiful young girl wearing a silk kimono, weeping because the river was swollen and she was unable to get across. The master bent down and picked her up, then waded across, carrying the girl in his arms.

When they reached the opposite bank, he set her down and the monks finished their journey in silence. That night the young monk, unable to restrain himself any longer, burst out, 'Master, why did you do that? It's against our vows to touch female flesh!'

'I let go of her on the other side of the river,' responded the master. 'Are you still carrying her?'

Inner purification

Meditation is a powerful medicine for the diseases of mind and body, and for sharpening our perceptive and creative abilities, but the real miracle of meditation lies in its power to bring about personal transformation and inner freedom.

In meditation we come into a direct relationship with our consciousness, often uncovering aspects of ourselves that have lain dormant or been suppressed for much of our lives. The first thing we confront when we turn our attention inwards is our own mind, with its outer covering of surface thoughts and non-stop chatter. Initially, this tissue of thoughts and inner gossip can seem impenetrable and quite overwhelming, which is why teachers of meditation have paid so much attention to how to deal with the mind in meditation and have come up with so many different methods. Using techniques of meditation, we learn to navigate our way through the mental haze of images, reverie and dialogue, and gradually become familiar with our inner landscape. Simultaneously, we start to delve deeper. As the broom of meditation sweeps under the carpet and into the corners, uncovering buried thoughts and emotions and deeply ingrained habits and prejudices, uncomfortable and sometimes intense feelings can arise. Strong feelings – loss, grief, hurt, anger and so on – that emerge during meditation often indicate that some form of emotional cleansing or mental clearance is going on. As they are processed and released, these emotions well up and flood our consciousness. Continuing with regular meditation and resisting the urge to suppress these feelings makes it easier to let them go and avoids our becoming submerged by them.

In this way a subtle process of inner purification takes place as meditation clears away layer upon layer of subconscious debris – the mental blocks, neuroses and false self-images we create for ourselves, the delusions of grandeur and the insecurities, the hopes, fears and suppressed emotions. As we become free of our inner demons we begin to operate from a different space – the open, uncluttered space of truth.

To bring about genuine and lasting personal transformation there is absolutely no substitute for regular meditation, combined with a conscious effort to integrate the insights and peace of mind that it fosters into your everyday life. This is why meditation teachers advise sitting quietly for a few minutes after meditation to allow the experience to infiltrate your entire being and help you maintain the awareness of it as you go about your day-to-day activities.

O how may I ever express that
    secret word?
O how can I say He is not like
    this, and He is like that?
If I say that He is within me,
    the universe is ashamed:
If I say that He is without me,
    it is falsehood.
He makes the inner and the outer
    worlds to be indivisibly one;
The conscious and the
    unconscious, both are His
    footstools.
He is neither manifest nor hidden,
    He is neither revealed nor
    unrevealed:
There are no words to tell that
    which He is.

Kabir

Spiritual enlightenment

The ultimate goal of meditation is not to become something, whether healthier, calmer or more spiritual, but to realize the truth of who and what we really are. The experience of the Self – the One, the Void, the Absolute, God, Supreme Awareness or whatever name we choose to give it – can occur spontaneously, perhaps triggered by music or nature. Most often, however, it is associated with spiritual practices, of which meditation is probably the most reliable.

Unquestionably, the ability to return to the Self over and over again, until it is imprinted on your consciousness and pervades your entire being, is the fruit of perseverance. Although the manifestation of the Self happens in its own time and can never be forced, meditation creates the optimum conditions. It stills the mind, and in that stillness the Self is revealed, much as an entire marine world becomes visible deep below the surface of clear waters when ripples subside.

Sages tell us that our essence is pure, timeless awareness, and that its nature is blissful. It is only our limited concept of ourselves – the idea that we are simply a body, a bundle of thoughts or a set of characteristics – that clouds our vision and prevents us from identifying with our true nature. Just as there is an infinite expanse of clear blue sky above the clouds, so beyond the clouds of thoughts, feelings and emotion that float across our inner screens is the limitless expanse of pure consciousness that is our essence. The purpose of meditation is to clean and polish the lens of our inner vision until it reflects us as we really are.

For if a mirror reflects not, of what use is it?

Knowest thou why thy mirror reflects not?

Because the rust has not been scoured from its face.

If it were purified from all rust and defilement,

It would reflect the shining of the sun of God.

Jalaluddin Rumi

Through meditation we become conscious of and familiar with our inner life: the mind and how it works. As we progress in meditation the mind becomes purified. Layers of thought and feeling, habit and conditioning, which control our lives and shroud our inner being, dissolve when they are brought into consciousness. As we shed previously unconscious desires, we begin to enjoy a greater sense of ease and inner tranquillity, often combined with a huge surge of energy. The inner chatter begins to subside and our identification with our bodies and minds loosens. Once we let go of the idea that we are a body or a mind, the Self – the pure awareness that is our essence – suddenly flashes forth, effortlessly, infusing us with a feeling of joy and exultation. We rest in the expanse of pure awareness and pulsating stillness that is our heart and source. Our limited sense of self merges into the infinite and we experience the essential unity of all things.

Because consciousness is by nature subjective, the mystical experience of the Self, in which we transcend ordinary consciousness and understand that we are the supreme reality, is not open to scientific verification. Transcendent states are never questioned by those who experience them, however, and are understood as imparting truths of a higher order of reality than our normal day-to-day experience of the world. A sense of recognition often accompanies these kinds of experience, however fleeting they may be – and even the briefest glimpse of the truth of our essential nature radically alters people's view of reality and often leads to dramatic changes in lifestyle.

Although mystical experience by its very nature defies description, sages have always found ways to point to the truth, and it is often hinted at through the lyrical poetry of ecstatics. The expression of their revelations in literature, art and scripture varies according to the culture through which they are filtered, yet mystical experience is a universal phenomena that lies at the heart of all religions. Enlightenment is a state of utter clarity but, because it is a union of opposites, all descriptions are full of seeming paradoxes. It is experienced as emptiness (the Void of Buddhism), yet is a full, and fulfilling, emptiness. It is complete stillness that nevertheless pulsates with energy. Subject and object, knower and known, merge, yet remain distinct. Above all, the Self is experienced as blissfulness and pure love.

The heart is the hub of all sacred places.
Go there and roam.   Bhagavan Nityananda

The heart of meditation

What a wonderful lotus it is, that blooms at the heart of
the spinning wheel of the universe! Only a few pure
souls know of its true delight.
Music is all around it, and there the heart partakes of the
joy of the Infinite Sea.
Kabir says: 'Dive thou into that Ocean of sweetness: thus
let all errors of life and of death flee away.'

Kabir

In many sacred traditions the heart is recognized as the
symbolic seat of enlightenment and love. It is the force of
love that draws us back into our source, and it is in the central
space of the heart that the great awakening takes place as we
come face to face with the Divine. The real spiritual journey
is this journey into our own hearts, culminating when we
are fully established in the awareness of the God or the Self.

Like the rose in Western culture, the lotus represents the spiritual centre,
or heart, in many Eastern traditions. The emergence of the beautiful
blossom from the muddy waters is symbolic of the spiritual seeker who
lives in the world, but remains untainted by it. The opening out of its
petals represents spiritual unfolding.

Meditation: Entering into the space of the heart

Read the meditation instructions through completely once or twice before you begin. You may find it helpful to record them, but be sure to leave plenty of space between each instruction. You may also find it helpful to set a timer for fifteen minutes, or longer if you are an experienced meditator.

Sit comfortably in any cross-legged position, or on a chair if you prefer with your legs uncrossed and your feet flat on the floor. Hold your back, head and neck erect yet relaxed. Tuck in your chin and place your hands in your lap or on your thighs. With the weight of your body centred over your sitting bones, feel these bones pressing down and your spine elongating, as though an invisible string were lifting you from the base of your spine through the crown of your head towards the ceiling. Placing a cushion beneath you to raise your hips will help keep the back in an upright position, increasing the flow of meditative energy circulating through the body.

Close your eyes and spend a few moments relaxing your body with the help of your breath, breathing in energy and breathing out tension. Then draw your awareness into the space of the heart – not the physical heart, but the subtle centre in the region of the physical heart where we experience emotions, especially love. Without disturbing the natural rhythm of your breath, breathe in and out of the heart centre, noting any feelings and sensations that come up. If you become aware that your attention has wandered away from the heart, gently draw it back to the centre, but without trying forcibly to push away thoughts.

Once you are centred in the space of the heart, feel yourself surrounded by love that is penetrating every pore of your being, from the outside in. As you continue breathing into your heart, be aware that you are breathing in love. As your breath flows out, feel the love at your centre radiating outwards from your heart into every particle of your body and enveloping the very stuff of your mind and consciousness until you are saturated with love.

Let any thoughts and feelings float in the love in and around you until eventually they merge into the vast ocean of love that is the underlying fabric of the universe.

At the end of your meditation open your eyes slowly and sit quietly for a few moments, absorbing the after-effects.

THE ROOTS of MEDITATION

2

Despite the differences in the names and forms used by the various religions, the ultimate truth to which they point is the same.   Dalai Lama

Since prehistory meditative practices have been used to awaken and unfold the innate spiritual potential lying dormant at the heart of every human. Written evidence for the practice of meditation is found in the Rig Veda, the most ancient of Indian texts, composed around the tenth century BC, but the earliest meditators were probably shamans, or witch doctors, of the Stone Age, who were believed to possess supernatural powers. These were acquired through ecstatic, trancelike states and used to heal, divine and make prophecies.

The intervening centuries have seen a variety of meditation techniques – ranging from the seemingly simple to the highly esoteric – evolve against a backdrop of different religious and philosophical systems. In spite of outer differences, the ultimate reality they allude to – whether called nirvana, God, the Absolute, the Void or Brahman – is in essence the same. Sacred traditions and the techniques of meditation they offer can be thought of as spiritual road maps marking out the pathways of the inner territory. There are highways and byways: some roads are fast and direct, others more circuitous and scenic, and some may appear to be dead ends. But all established traditions and their practices bring us closer to the truth and help to align us with the flow of grace. The paths we tread and find ourselves attracted to are determined by the culture we are part of, our personalities and even fate. Despite its religious and metaphysical roots, however, the actual practice of meditation does not necessarily involve the acceptance of any beliefs.

In fact, although meditation is commonly taught within the framework of religious or philosophical beliefs, these are best put to one side during meditation, which is about the direct experience of truth rather than indoctrination with a belief system. Meditation cuts through conflicting beliefs and pierces to the very heart of religion. Traditions and techniques exist to take us to the gateway of the inner realm and open the door into the core of our being, the space where we come face to face with Truth, by whatever name we choose to call it.

The diversity of sacred traditions, and the unity at their essence, was illustrated by the nineteenth-century Indian mystic Ramakrishna with a parable about the clear, colourless, tasteless liquid with which we quench our thirst and which is essential to all life. In Hindi it is called *pani*. The same liquid is called water in English or *agua* in Spanish. Just as it is given a different name in each language, so each culture uses a different vessel to drink from and to store the liquid, which adapts perfectly to the shape of whatever container it is found in. These impart a different character or flavour to the experience of drinking. Yet regardless of the name we give it and the shape in which we contain it, we all draw from the same inexhaustible well. There are people from all traditions – Christian or Moslem, Buddhist or Hindu alike – who have attained the highest knowledge. These enlightened souls tell us that God cannot be found in temples or through rituals and ceremonies, nor through any amount of study. The ultimate truth lies within us, and can be known only through direct experience.

Often the only way to discover the path best suited to us is by a process of trial and error, but constant chopping and changing routes can mean you make slow – or no – progress. Spiritual development is not about collecting more and more information on different spiritual teachings to add to your repertoire. It is about bringing the teachings to life through your own experience of putting them into practice.

This section of the book describes briefly the traditions within which meditation plays a major part and from which nearly all meditation techniques are drawn, whether for relaxing and boosting health, as a form of self-development or for spiritual enlightenment. A disproportionate number of these traditions are Eastern, since historically the practice of

This 13th century Japanese Buddha, seated in the lotus position, has his thumb and forefinger held together in a gesture of concentration.

meditation has been more widespread in the East. India has a special role as the birthplace of several major world religions and home to many more, and has spawned a huge and colourful diversity of practices. For many people, India is still the spiritual heartland of meditation and place of all pilgrimage, despite the proliferation of Western retreats, ashrams and zendos. Ultimately, however, the real spiritual journey is the inner one. As the spiritual teacher and philosopher Jiddu Krishnamurti once said, enlightenment is where you are.

Yoga is ecstasy.

Vyasa, 5th century Indian sage

This stone seal found at Mohenjo-Daro, where the ancient Indus Valley

civilization flourished, is one of the earliest known portrayals of a yogi.

Most of us associate yoga, and particularly hatha yoga, with the system of physical postures that are now so widely taught as a form of physical fitness in health clubs and gymnasiums, community centres and church halls. In fact, hatha yoga, which is devoted to the purification and strengthening of the body through a combination of physical exercises, breathing techniques and cleansing practices, is just one branch of a labyrinthine tree and the physical aspect of hatha yoga is traditionally regarded as preparatory to the more meditative techniques employed in its more advanced practice. The venerable and very fruitful tree of yoga, which continues to sprout new branches and offshoots, offers an extraordinarily diverse collection of tools and techniques for self-transformation and spiritual development.

Yoga

Yoga is a very ancient and highly sophisticated spiritual tradition that originated in India five thousand years ago. The earliest archaeological evidence for the practice of yoga is found in a number of soapstone seals dating back to the third millennium BC, discovered during excavations on the site of Mohenjo-Daro in the Indus Valley. One of these depicts a figure identified as the god Shiva, the mythological founder of yoga, seated on a throne in a yogic posture. Shiva is associated with Hinduism, but the practice of yoga is found in, and has influenced, all the great religious traditions originating in India – Hinduism, Buddhism, Jainism and Sikhism. Yoga has also inspired the various offshoots of these traditions, including Zen and Tibetan Buddhism. Although it is often taught and practised within the context of one or other of these, yoga is nevertheless best thought of as spiritual technology rather than religion, requiring practical application and know-how rather than belief. Its methods can be used within the framework of any religion.

Because it is such a multifaceted system of spiritual disciplines, yoga is very hard to define. The word 'yoga' is usually translated as 'union' – the union of the individual self with the supreme Self or God – and shares the same Sanskrit root as the English 'yoke'. Since any path to this fundamental unity may be called yoga, many branches of yoga have arisen within Hinduism embracing the various ways in which this union is achieved. These different paths of yoga are not opposed. Rather they overlap, combine and intertwine like the strands of a rope. In its broadest sense yoga is simply a pathway to knowledge of ultimate reality or God. Both the Indian guru and the Christian mystic are yogis in this sense, which transcends the barriers of culture and sectarianism.

When the five senses and the mind are still, and reason rests in silence, then begins the Path Supreme. This calm steadiness of the senses is called yoga.   *Katha Upanishad*

The earliest written reference to the yogic practices of India is found in the *Vedas*, a collection of hymns composed between 2000 and 3000 BC that were transmitted orally long before they were written down. However it was not until the *Upanishads*, which followed the *Vedas*, that the teachings of yoga become more explicit. The teachings of the *Upanishads* are known as *Vedanta*, meaning 'the end of the Vedas', and the Upanishadic sages considered meditation to be the chief means to enlightenment. Yogic practices explored in the Upanishads include *raja yoga*, the royal path to self-realization through posture, breath control, concentration and meditation, *mantra yoga*, the path to self-realization through repetition of sacred sounds and syllables, *hatha yoga*, the path to self-realization based on purification of the physical body, and *laya yoga*, the path to self-realization through absorption of the mind in inner sounds and lights. Closely associated with hatha yoga is *kundalini yoga*, the path to self-realization through arousal of our latent spiritual power. All of these have a role to play within *tantric yoga*, a controversial approach to enlightenment because it also involves worship of the female principle in the form of the goddess Shakti (the consort of Shiva) and ritual sexuality, either literal or symbolic.

The best known, and most popular, literature of both yoga and Hinduism is the *Bhagavad Gita* (Song of God), written around the sixth century BC. The *Gita* takes the form of a dialogue between the god Krishna and the warrior Prince Arjuna on the eve of battle, and deals with the very real issue of how to balance worldly responsibilities with spiritual goals. It describes three main paths of yoga: *jnana yoga*, the path of knowledge and wisdom, *karma yoga*, the path to self-realization through selfless action, and *bhakti yoga*, the path of devotion to God. The *Gita* brought yoga away from the realm of the purely ascetic, offering a practical spiritual teaching for everyone.

The most significant influence in the history of yoga was the *Yoga Sutra* of the sage Patanjali, who compiled and systematized the principles of yoga in the second century, giving it its classical format. Because of this it is often known as Classical Yoga. Patanjali's yoga system has become equated with *raja yoga*, the royal path of meditation, mentioned above. A more detailed description follows, along with descriptions of the other main forms of yoga and how meditation is practised within them. These various types of yoga complement one another and in practice it is unusual to follow one form of yoga exclusively.

The Hindu deity Shiva, considered the arch-yogin and ascetic, is often depicted with long matted hair, smeared with ashes and wearing a garland of skulls, all signs of his renunciation. The crescent moon in his hair symbolizes mystical knowledge and the serpent coiled around his neck represents the *kundalini*, the inner spiritual potential. He sits upon a tiger skin, representing his power, and holds a trident, which symbolizes the three primary constituents of nature – lucidity, energy and inertia – from whose interaction the entire universe is created.

Yoga is the stilling of the waves of consciousness.   Patanjali

Raja yoga

Raja yoga, or royal yoga, is the name given to the system of yoga described in the second century by Patanjali in his *Yoga Sutra*. Patanjali's main concern in the Sutras is the mapping of a practical way to achieve spiritual enlightenment, which is achieved in his system through a graduated series of practices. The most important of these is meditation, the preliminary stages being intended as preparation for the higher stages of concentration and meditation. Patanjali's system of yoga is also known as *ashtanga yoga* (not to be confused with the strenuous form of hatha yoga currently in vogue), referring to the eight steps of this path to self-transcendence. These are:

1   **Ethical rules (*yama*)**

The five moral obligations or restraints that form the framework of yoga and that are common to most religions are: not to harm (*ahimsa*), truthfulness (*satya*), not to steal (*asteya*), chastity or not to lust (*brahmacharya*) and not to be greedy or possessive (*aparigrahah*).

2   **Observances (*niyama*)**

The five observances or disciplines that prepare the practitioner for yogic training are: purity (*shauca*), contentment (*santosha*), austerity (*tapas*), study (*svadhyaya*) and devotion or surrender to God or Supreme Reality, however we may conceive it (*isvara pranidhana*).

These first two steps underpin all forms of yoga.

3   **Posture (*asana*)**

Asana is Sanskrit for seat, an indication that the range of yoga postures we are now so familiar with developed from the positions used for sitting in meditation. For Patanjali, *asana* almost certainly refers primarily to meditation postures, since a comfortable and stable position that can be held steadily is essential for prolonged meditation.

4   **Breath control (*pranayama*)**

Prana is the life force that permeates the individual through the breath, though it is more than the breath, which is simply its gross manifestation. *Prana* and consciousness are intimately connected and through *pranayama*, or breath control, yogis energize the body-mind, stimulate the flow of the life force and prepare the mind for meditation. The practice of *pranayama* involves regulating the incoming and outgoing flow of breath, and includes the suspension or retention of breath between the inspiration and expiration. During meditation itself breathing is normally allowed to come and go naturally, unless *pranayama* and breath retention occur spontaneously.

5   **Sense withdrawal (*pratyahara*)**

The practice of meditation posture and breath control leads to the withdrawal of the senses from external stimuli and the turning inward of one's attention (*pratyahara*). The moment we close our eyes and look within, however,

we are confronted with all sorts of internal stimuli –
tensions, tummy rumbles, discomfort in our backs and
joints – not to mention the activity going on in our minds,
which can be filled with very unruly thoughts! So the next
step is to focus the mind using concentration techniques.

6 Concentration (*dharana*)

Following on the process of sensory withdrawal is the
practice of fixing the attention on a single point or focus
(*dharana*). This can range from the tip of one's nose to
the vast expanse of the sky. Or attention may be focussed
on an object such as a candle, flower or the image of a
deity, placed a convenient distance away and gazed at. After
a while the eyes can be closed and the object internalized
and held in the mind's eye. Alternatively you may choose
an internal focus for one-pointed attention such as a
mantra, the heart centre or one of the other chakras
(energy centres, see page 64–65), or the flow of your breath.

7 Meditation (*dhyana*)

Meditation is defined by Patanjali as the continuous flow
of attention towards the object of concentration – in other
words the merging of the mind and its object. This total
immersion, or flowing of the mind, into a single focus to
the exclusion of all else is the point at which dhyana or
meditation arises and the yogi enters a different state of
consciousness.

8 Ecstasy (*samadhi*)

As when concentration leads to meditation, so when all
the waves or movements of the mind are stilled through
meditation the yogi experiences *samadhi* or ecstasy. The
last three steps – concentration, meditation and ecstasy –
when practised successively form a continuous process
known as *samyama*.

A by-product of *samyama* is the acquisition of supernatural powers that are evidence of the yogi's progress.
Patanjali devotes an entire chapter to describing the various powers – such as knowledge of the past and present,
the ability to read the minds of others and so on – but
warns against the dangers of using them. These occult
powers are said to distract the yogi and to be an obstacle
on the road to full enlightenment.

In Patanjali's system, concentration is the focussing of attention on a chosen region, point or object, inside or outside the
body. Meditation is the state of absorption that arises from an
uninterrupted flow of attention towards such an object so that
the object fills the entire field of consciousness. Thus concentration leads to meditation, which in turn leads to ecstasy.
Typical focal points include the chakras, feelings and emotions, the visualization of light, the tip of the nose, the flame
of a candle or the image of a deity – the list is endless.
Chapter 3, 'The Practical Art of Meditation', includes many
techniques that are in accord with Patanjali's yoga.

Brahman (*ultimate reality*) is mantra. *Rig Veda*

Mantra yoga

Sound, originating as a vibration, not only shapes our individual consciousness, but is said to be the creative force underlying the evolution of the entire universe. It is this creative power of sound that is the basis of mantra yoga, the path to enlightenment through mantra repetition.

The power of sound to affect consciousness has been recognized since the earliest times. We experience it in everyday life through language, music, the sounds around us and even the 'sound' of silence. A Bach cantata can transport us into a sublime state, while the scraping sound of chalk on a blackboard makes our flesh creep. Words – a potent combination of sound and meaning – have the ability to literally transform our inner reality. Potentially devastating when used against us, language also has the power to change our entire mindset for the better. This is the basis of positive thinking. Destructive and limiting thoughts in the form of little voices inside that tell us we are losers or not good enough in myriad different (untrue!) ways are consciously replaced by positive, expansive messages, otherwise known as affirmations.

Mantra, meaning 'an instrument for thinking', is a tool used to transform the mind. Another definition of mantra is 'that which protects or saves the mind', so a mantra can be thought of as protecting us and leading to our salvation. In practice, a mantra is a sacred sound, word or phrase that can be chanted aloud, recited quietly or repeated mentally. Although it is physically expressed as sound, the real essence of a mantra is the soundless vibration of the divine energy embedded within it.

Because it is an expression of ultimate reality, consciously repeating a mantra charges us with the subtle vibrations of its energy and links us to higher consciousness. To awaken the transformative potency of a mantra through one's own efforts can, however, take many years of dedicated practice. A mantra is said to bear full fruit only when it is empowered by and received from an enlightened teacher, when its effectiveness is multiplied many times over.

A mantra works by focussing the mind and drawing the attention inwards, leading to progressively higher and more subtle levels of consciousness. Silent repetition of a mantra, popularized by the Maharishi Mahesh Yogi's system of Transcendental Meditation®, is one of the most widespread techniques of meditation and is said to be the easiest approach to enlightenment in the current age.

The sacred syllable *om*, here boldly written in red on a white wall in Kutch, India, is the best known

of all mantras and is said to be the primordial sound or vibration from which the entire universe

arises. *Om* symbolizes the Absolute, both in its creative, or manifest, dimension and in its

unmanifest dimension, represented by the dot or *bindu*, which adds a nasal quality to the *m*.

Om is said to have existed since the beginning of creation and to have been revealed to sages in

deepest meditation. It is used at the beginning and end of Indian prayers in much the same way

as the Christian *Amen*, and as a mantra either on its own or when used in combination with other

syllables and words, adding to their power.

Hatha yoga

When people say that they do yoga they are usually talking
about the physical postures that have become one of the
biggest health trends in the last decade. Hatha yoga is taught
everywhere and has spawned so many offshoots of its own
that most health clubs and yoga centres now offer more than
one type.

What is often not fully appreciated is that hatha yoga is
part of a wider spiritual system, the path to self-realization
through the purification of the physical and subtle bodies.
The subtle body, discussed in detail on pages 63–65, is central
to hatha yoga. Essentially it is an invisible, energetic body
roughly corresponding to the physical body through which
the life force circulates by means of a network of channels
and centres. Ultimately, through bringing together and harmo-
nizing the physical and subtle aspects of the body, hatha yoga
aims to awaken and activate the *kundalini*, the psychospiritual
energy said to lie dormant at the base of the spine.

Hatha yoga comprises the first four steps of raja yoga (see
page 52), and the practice of *asanas* (postures) has always
been considered important for meditators as it helps to establish a steady base for meditation and strengthens the body.
Enlightenment is both a physical and a mental event, and the
practice of hatha yoga enables the body to withstand the full
force of the transcendental state. Yet although hatha yoga is
classically seen as a preparation for the later meditative stages
of raja yoga (the *Hatha Yoga Pradipika*, the main literature of
the hatha yoga tradition, states that 'All means of hatha yoga

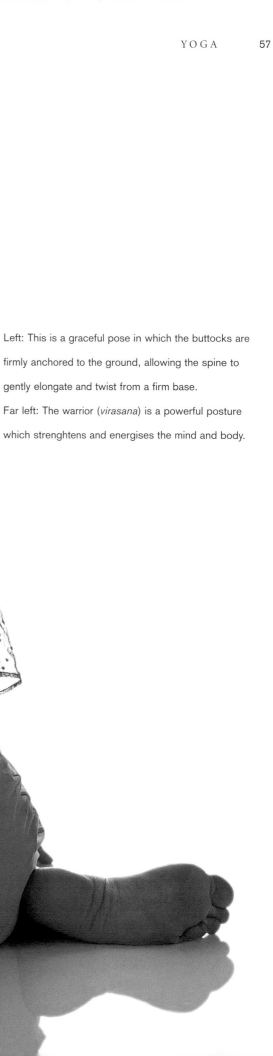

Left: This is a graceful pose in which the buttocks are firmly anchored to the ground, allowing the spine to gently elongate and twist from a firm base.

Far left: The warrior (*virasana*) is a powerful posture which strenghtens and energises the mind and body.

are for reaching perfection in raja yoga'), its true practice
involves intense meditation. The characteristic technique of
meditation in hatha yoga – as in tantric yoga – is visualization
(see pages 157–171). Meditators usually begin with a 'coarse'
object, such as a lighted candle, and progress to increasingly
subtle objects such as the chakras, as described and illustrated
on page 170. Eventually, no external object is needed.

Like other forms of yoga, hatha yoga is underpinned by
the practices of *yama* and *niyama* (see page 52), which serve
to foster ethical behaviour and purify the mind. If this ethical
framework is neglected and no form of meditation is practised, as tends to happens in the West, the practice of hatha
yoga can become little more than a form of physical fitness.
Nevertheless, many people who first turn to yoga to relieve
stress or tone up their bodies find they tap into a new kind of
experience – a pleasurable sense of physical liberation that
simultaneously draws the attention inwards. The practice of
hatha yoga should incorporate the mind and spirit as well as
the body through a combination of breath control, postures
and a meditative approach. One way to do this is to fuse your
whole attention with your body as you practise, and/or to
visualize the perfect performance of any given *asana* as you
move into it. Hatha yoga postures are nothing less than meditation in action when practised in this way. When the body is
moved with the breath, and brought into perfect alignment,
the body becomes a temple and its movements the expression
of spirit flowing through it.

The body is my temple and asanas are my prayers.

B.K.S. Iyengar

Above: The revolving head-to-knee pose (*paravrtta janu sirsasana*) is an advanced yoga position in which the body is extended over one leg and turned so that the back of the head rests on the knee.

Left: The triangle pose (*trikonasana*), so-named because of the shapes of the spaces formed by the body in this position, is suitable for beginners.

Schools of hatha yoga

Some of the better-known schools of hatha yoga are:

Iyengar yoga Probably the most established school of yoga worldwide, this is a slow, structured and very precise form of yoga devised by B.K.S. Iyengar, now in his eighties and widely recognized as a driving influence behind the spread of yoga to the West. A variety of props – blocks, bolsters, straps and ropes – are used in Iyengar classes to assist students in achieving the correct alignment of the body and the risk of injury is minimal.

Sivananda yoga A school of yoga with centres around the world established by Swami Vishnu Devananda at the request of his guru Swami Sivananda. A gentle approach to yoga that nevertheless achieves high standards, classes are based on a core series of twelve postures and their variations, which are always performed in the same sequence. Correct breathing, relaxation and a meditative approach are integral to the practice of Sivananda yoga.

Ashtanga yoga A fast-paced, athletic and physically demanding form of yoga that takes its name from the eight (*ashta*) limbs (*anga*) of Patanjali's eightfold system, but in practice has little in common with it. The best-known proponent of this form of yoga is Patabhi Jois, whose teacher was Krishnamacharya, the modern yoga master who was also Iyengar's teacher and brother-in-law. Ashtanga yoga tends to

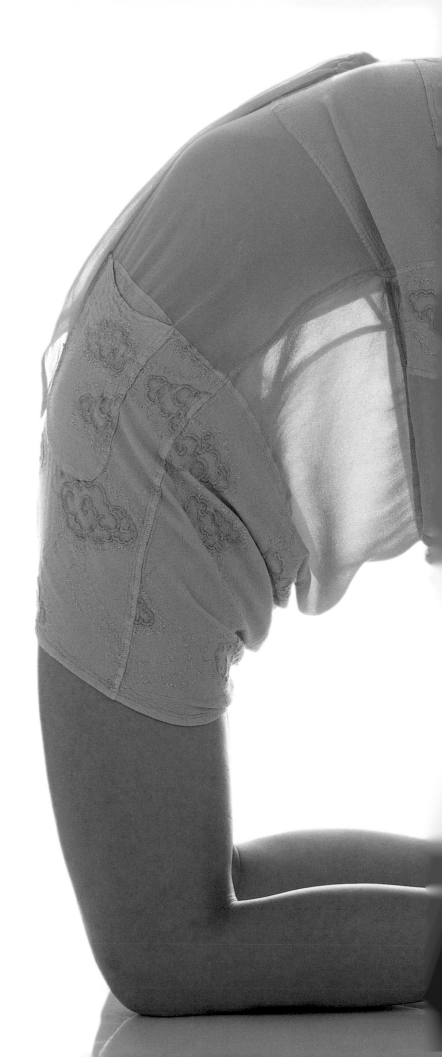

In the camel pose (*ustrasana*) the spine arches back while the hips press forward.

attract people looking for an intelligent approach to keeping fit and improving their bodies, including more than its fair share of celebrities and a lot of highly competitive professionals. From here many discover yoga is having a more profound effect on them than pounding the treadmill or other staples of the gym, and go on to explore the meditative aspects of yoga. Ashtanga is an excellent system that gets good results when properly taught, but it has a higher rate of injury than other more gentle forms of yoga and is best avoided if you have any physical injuries or are unfit.

Bikram yoga Developed by Bikram Choudry, who became the youngest ever National Yoga Champion of India at the age of twelve. A serious injury caused by a weightlifting accident encouraged him to develop his own series of twenty-six yoga postures, which are performed in sequence, as part of his recovery. Bikram Choudry moved his headquarters to Beverly Hills in the 1980s and his style of yoga has now become hugely popular, especially with celebrities. This 'Guru of the Stars' is said to lead a pretty ritzy lifestyle himself, but is acknowledged as a master of hatha yoga asanas. Best known for being practised by scantily clad aficionados in a room heated to 108°F (48°C) – which allows the muscles to stretch further and encourages sweating and the release of toxins – Bikram yoga is also known as 'hot' or 'sweaty yoga'. A Bikram yoga class is a tough workout and not for the faint-hearted.

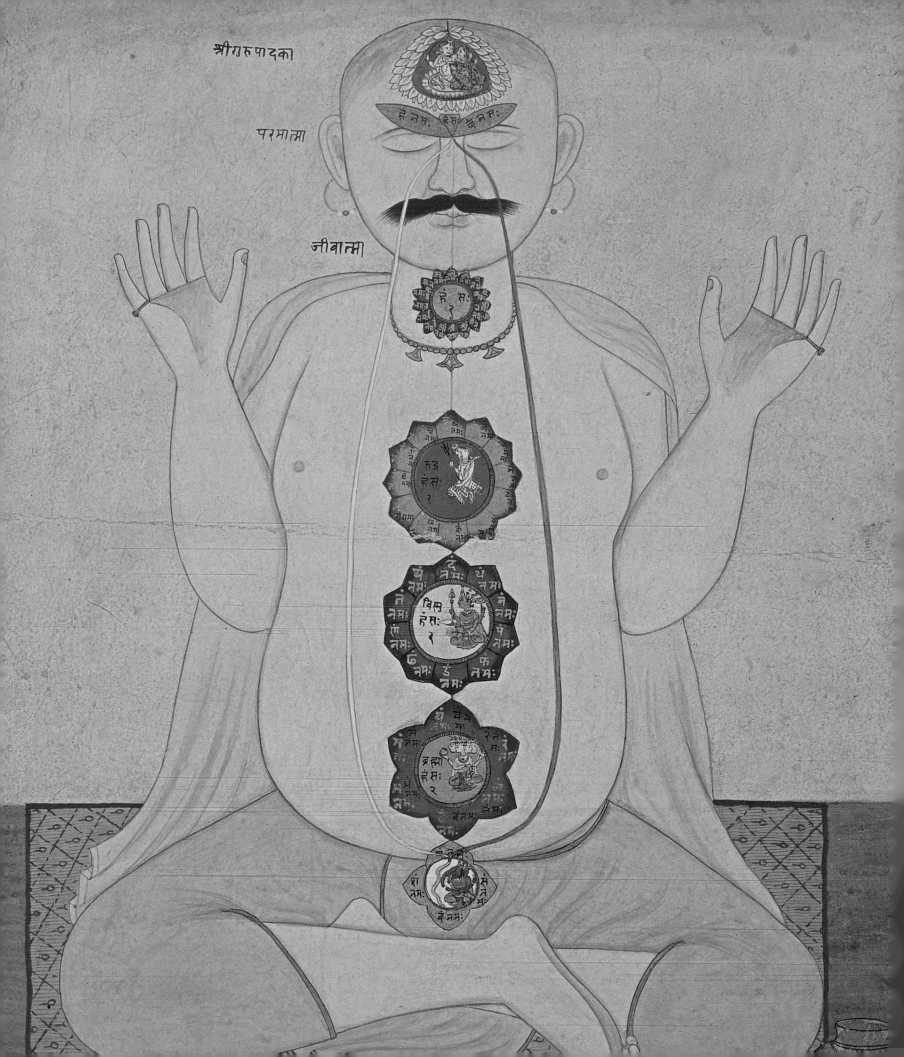

The subtle body

The practices of hatha, laya, kundalini and tantric yoga are all based on the idea that there is a subtle counterpart to the physical body. This body, known as the 'subtle body', is essentially a network of energy currents or channels (*nadis*) and energy centres (*chakras*). The chakras may be more or less highly charged, more or less active, and are said to reflect both our physical health and our spiritual state. The energy that comprises and flows through the subtle body is known as *prana*, meaning 'life force', which is externally manifested as the breath, although it is not identical with it. This universal energy is variously known as *chi* (by the Chinese), *ki* (Japanese) and *mana* (Polynesian). Kabbalists referred to it as the astral light while the psychiatrist Wilhelm Reich coined the term 'orgone'.

The principal channel is the *sushumna*, which runs along the spine, extending from the perineum to the crown of the head. All the major chakras are located along this spinal axis. On either side of the sushumna are two other important channels, the *ida* and *pingala*, which wind around the *sushumna* in a spiral resembling a caduceus. They criss-cross at the main chakras, with the exception of the *sahasrara*, and extend from the base of the spine to the midpoint between the eyebrows, or 'third eye', ending at the opening of the two nostrils.

In the normal course of events, the life force flows up and down the ida and pingala, and the chakras assimilate, transform and redirect this energy throughout the body. So long as prana is oscillating between the ida and pingala, attention is directed outwards. The purpose of the postures and breathing techniques of hatha yoga, and the spiritual practices of laya, kundalini and tantric yoga, is to force the flow of prana along the sushumna. This arouses the dormant kundalini energy, stimulates the chakras and focusses the attention within.

This early 19th century illustration from Himachal Pradesh in India shows the principle chakras and channels of the subtle body.

Sahasrara

Ajna

Vishuddha

Anahata

Manipura

Svadhisthana

Muladhara

The seven principal chakras

The chakras are arranged vertically along the sushumna, the main energy channel, and roughly correspond with nerve centres in the physical body such as in the solar plexus. Richly symbolic and colourful, the chakras are depicted as lotuses, each with a different number of petals determined by the number and position of the nadis around it. Each chakra has a different vibration and is associated with different mantras, elements and functions. Each also has its own deities, representing different manifestations of God. From the base up, the chakras can be summarized as follows:

Muladhara The 'root' chakra is situated at the perineum, just in front of the anus, and symbolized as a lotus with four petals. This is the seat of the dormant kundalini, depicted as a (female) serpent coiled three and a half times around a lingam or phallus, her mouth closing the entrance to the sushumna. The chakra is associated with the earth element, the elephant (symbolizing strength) and the mantra *lam*. The presiding deities are Brahma (the Creator) and the goddess Dakini. Meditation on the kundalini shining within this lotus is said to bring mastery of speech, the acquisition of all kinds of learning, freedom from disease and great happiness.

Svadhisthana Located at the genitals, this chakra is symbolized as a lotus with six petals. The chakra is associated with the element of water, a white alligator (symbolizing fertility) and the mantra *vam*. The presiding deities are Vishnu and

Rakini. Meditation on this lotus is said to destroy the six enemies – lust, anger, greed, delusion, pride and envy, to free one from ignorance and to bring knowledge.

Manipura Located at the navel, this chakra is symbolized as a lotus with ten petals, and is so-named because it is lustrous as a jewel. The chakra is associated with the fire element, the ram (symbolizing passion or fiery energy) and the mantra *ram*. The presiding deities are Rudra and Lakini. Meditation on this lotus is said to bring about the power to destroy and create, and all the wealth of knowledge is acquired.

Anahata Located at the heart, this chakra is symbolized as a lotus with twelve petals and is named after the 'unstruck' or transcendental sound, which is said to be heard in the heart. The chakra is associated with the air element, a black antelope (symbolizing speed) and the mantra *yam*. The presiding deities are Isha and Kakini. This lotus is likened to a wish-fulfilling tree and meditation on it is said to bring great benefits including the power to create, protect and destroy, steadiness of mind and great powers of concentration, complete control of all the senses, prosperity and great good fortune.

Vishuddha Located at the base of the throat, this chakra is symbolized as a lotus with sixteen petals and is called 'pure' because meditation on this chakra brings freedom from impurity. The chakra is associated with the element ether, a snow-white elephant (symbolizing purity and strength) and the mantra *ham*. The presiding deities are Sadashiva and Shakini. The vishuddha chakra is the gateway to liberation for those who have purified and gained control over their senses and meditation on this lotus is said to bring eloquence, wisdom, peace of mind, knowledge of past, present and future, freedom from all vices and from disease and sorrow.

Ajna The 'third eye', located between the eyebrows, is symbolized as a lotus with two petals. It is the 'command' chakra, through which the yogi receives the command of the guru or teacher, communicated telepathically. The chakra is associated with the mantra *om*, the presiding deities are Shiva and Hakini, and it is the location of the subtle mind. Through meditation on this lotus the yogi is said to realize his or her unity with the Absolute and enjoy uninterrupted bliss. Paranormal powers such as omniscience are acquired.

Sahasrara This chakra is known as the 'thousand-petalled' lotus, and is situated at the crown of the head. This resplendent centre represents the flowering of all spiritual practices: the seat of full enlightenment and absolute bliss. The yogi who has knowledge of the sahasrara is liberated from the cycle of birth and rebirth and achieves complete freedom.

Kundalini is the basis of all yoga tantras. All yogas are attainable by the awakening of kundalini. Swami Muktananda

Kundalini yoga

Kundalini, symbolically represented by a coiled serpent lying at the base of the spine, is the latent spiritual power that lies dormant in all human beings. Arousing the sleeping kundalini transforms and expands individual consciousness and all the spiritual practices of kundalini yoga are directed to this end. Once activated – and this may occur spontaneously or through various processes of initiation, as well as through self-effort and spiritual disciplines – the kundalini is often referred to as *shakti*, the primordial energy or creative power. Until this awakening occurs it is said that no real spiritual progress can be made. Once shakti is activated, the mind is drawn inwards. Meditation happens quite naturally as the shakti travels along the vast network of subtle pathways in the body known as *nadis*, sweeping them clean and purifying the mind and body in preparation for higher states of consciousness.

Kundalini awakening was virtually unheard of in the West before the 1970s, but during the hippie era, and the rebirth of spiritual values it ushered in, people began to experiment with different spiritual disciplines. More people became aware of what the kundalini was and there were more reports of people experiencing the phenomena associated with an active kundalini: spontaneous movements, gestures and postures, altered breathing patterns, sensations of energy flowing through the spine and other parts of the body, intense feelings of heat or cold, inner sounds and lights, visions, psychic powers, ecstacy and other mystical illumination. One of the best documented accounts of kundalini awakening was provided by Gopi Krishna (who meditated for three hours every morning over a period of seventeen years), in his book *Kundalini: The Evolutionary Energy in Man* (1967):

'Suddenly, with a roar like that of a waterfall, I felt a stream of liquid light entering my brain through the spinal cord... The illumination grew brighter and brighter, the roaring louder, I experienced a rocking sensation and then felt myself slipping out of my body, entirely enveloped in a halo of light.'

An equally dramatic account was given by Swami Muktananda in his autobiography, *Play of Consciousness* (1970):

'I sat down on my asana [seat] and immediately went into the lotus posture. All around me I saw flames spreading. The whole universe was on fire. A burning ocean had burst open and swallowed up the whole earth. An army of ghosts and demons surrounded me. All the while I was locked tight in the lotus posture, my eyes closed, my chin pressed down against my throat so that no air could escape. Then I felt a searing pain in the knot of nerves in the muladhara, situated at the base of the spine.'

This statue of coiled snakes symbolizing the kundalini can be seen in the grounds of the Kanchipuram temple in Tamil Nadu, southern India.

Men and women ritually bathe at the Shiva lingam altar at the Gai Ghat along the Ganges River in Varanasi, India. The kundalini is coiled around the *lingam*, or phallus, that symbolises the creative principle. In man the dormant kundalini is depicted coiled around an inner lingam in the muladhara chakra, at the base of the spine.

The art of arousing the kundalini and channelling the tremendous energy released is highly developed in yoga, but kundalini is a universal principle known under different names and described in esoteric teachings the world over. It was known about in ancient Egypt and China, although it remained a jealously guarded secret. References to kundalini-type experiences can be found in Kabbalistic, Hermetic, Rosicrucian and Masonic writings as well as in the works of Plato and other Greek philosophers. They are also found amongst some Native Americans and the !Kung bushmen of Africa, who dance for hours on end to awaken the N'Um (kundalini) power, which rises from the base of the spine to the skull and transports them into a mystical state that can be used for healing purposes. Poets also sometimes allude to the supreme reality the awakened kundalini reveals, in ways that go over the head of anyone who is not awakened.

Kundalini awakening can be confusing and even terrifying for the unprepared, so kundalini yoga is best undertaken under the guidance of an enlightened teacher. It employs many of the techniques of hatha yoga, together with the use of mantras and visualization of the main chakras or energy centres that lie along the *sushumna*, the central pathway of the subtle body that runs along the spine, from the base of the spine to the crown of the head (see pages 64–65). The kundalini is classically depicted as rising through the *sushumna*, piercing the chakras (symbolized as lotus flowers, each having different numbers of petals) and completing its journey in the sahasrara

(the thousand-petalled lotus at the crown of the head), bathing the yogi with radiant light. The aim of the yogi is to raise the kundalini energy to the sahasrara as often as possible. When it becomes stabilized in this chakra the yogi is enlightened. The awakened kundalini is an intelligent force that in practice moves around in a less linear fashion than described in the classic model, driving the yogi's spiritual evolution in whatever way is most appropriate to him or her.

Laya yoga

This is one of the more esoteric forms of yoga. Central to its practice is the awakening and manipulation of the kundalini. Laya yoga can be thought of as the higher, meditative stage of hatha yoga, with which it shares practices such as *pranayama*, or breath control. It is closely associated with kundalini yoga and tantric yoga.

Laya yoga literally means the yoga of absorption or dissolution, and involves meditation on the chakras and their symbolism (see pages 64–65 and 170) in a prescribed fashion. Once the kundalini is activated, various inner sounds and lights may manifest, various forms of pranayama may occur spontaneously and breathing may become shallow or imperceptible. Through absorption in such inner phenomena, all mental activity dissolves. The laya yogi transcends the limitations of everyday consciousness and achieves self-realization.

Tantric yoga

Tantra is a movement that arose within both Hinduism and Buddhism in the middle of the first millennium, marking a radical shift away from the asceticism that characterized other approaches to spirituality current in India at the time. Tantric teachers took the Vedantic philosophy of non-duality to its logical conclusion, taking the view that if there is only one Self or Reality there is nothing to be gained by self-denial and the renunciation of worldly pleasures. Tantra finds no incompatibility between the sensual and the spiritual, and sexual symbolism is used extensively.

Tantra, 'that by which knowledge is extended', is above all an intensely practical approach to enlightenment, which is seen as a physical as well as mental and spiritual experience. The practices of yoga – particularly mantra yoga, laya yoga and kundalini yoga – are central to achieving it. The postures of hatha yoga not only strengthen the physical body, but more importantly from the perspective of tantra they work on the subtle body, stimulating the various energy centres or chakras and opening up the subtle pathways or currents. Awakening the kundalini or divine energy is central to tantric yoga and this is achieved through various kinds of meditation using mantras (see pages 147–151), mudras (physical gestures), visualization of the chakras (see pages 68–69 and 170) and mystical diagrams known as yantras (see over and page 166). These are similar to the mandalas of Tibetan Buddhism (see pages 82–83 and 166–169) and are shown in many Tantric works of art.

Goddess-worship lies at the heart of Tantra and, once activated, the kundalini energy is often known as *shakti*, the cosmic creative power, and represented as a goddess. The culmination of the Tantric yogi's spiritual journey – transcendental ecstacy – is represented as the union of the god Shiva and his consort Shakti. The couple, so absorbed in one another that they are no longer aware of any differences between them, symbolize the non-dual nature of ultimate reality. Sexual union is the chief symbol of Tantra and the introduction of ritual sexuality – enacted literally by some – was highly controversial and caused Tantra to come into some disrepute both in India and the West. Tantra became synonymous with 'sacred' sex, conjuring up images of wild and elaborate rituals. However, sex is not regarded as an end in itself in Tantra nor is orgasm its climax. In fact the male participant is supposed to prevent the discharge of semen, the flow of which is then reversed in an alchemical process, transforming it into a spiritual energy that accelerates the yogi's spiritual evolution. Thanks to more liberal attitudes, greater understanding and the pioneering work of a few individuals, Tantra is now recognized as a sophisticated system of practical teachings for spiritual development.

Sculptures on a frieze on the Chitragupta Temple in Khajuraho, India,
showing a couple engaging in the ritual sexuality which is a feature of
Tantric yoga, whether enacted symbolically or literally.

Shri yantra

A *yantra* is a mystical diagram, a symbolic representation of the creative process of evolution, the unfolding of the phenomenal world. The central point of a yantra is called the *bindu* and represents the potential energy that is the origin of the unfolded reality of our everyday experience. Through meditation on a yantra (which involves internalizing the yantra in its entirety and reconstructing it mentally, and is one of the techniques used in tantric meditation), the yogi reverses the process of evolution. Through this act of meditative involution the distinctions between subject and object disappear, and the yogi experiences the ecstacy of union with the Absolute.

The most important of all yantras is the Shri yantra, made up of the bindu or potential energy symbolized as a white dot and a series of triangles that express the process of divine expansion, how the One becomes many. The first of these triangles is a red, downward-pointing triangle symbolizing the female power (*shakti*). From this original couple, the white bindu and the first red triangle, evolve nine interwoven triangles: four white upward-pointing ones representing the male cosmic principle (*Shiva*) and four more red downward-pointing ones representing the female principal. The interpenetration of these nine triangles produces a total of forty-three smaller triangles that express the subdivisions of divine energy. The symbolism of the rings of lotus petals is twofold, representing both the unfolded reality of the world and the spiritual unfolding of the individual, the knowledge of the Absolute that is said to be revealed in the mystical space within the depths of the heart.

Meditation should form the basis for action. Dalai Lama

The yogas of the *Bhagavad Gita*

The *Bhagavad Gita*, the great Indian epic, takes the form of a conversation between the much-loved Indian god Krishna, who has taken human form, and his pupil Prince Arjuna. Krishna explains the teachings of yoga and its various paths, offering an approach to spiritual life that can be followed by anyone. Although meditation plays a part in all of these forms of yoga, it is in a less explicit way than in the yogas described previously. However, no description of yoga would be complete without mentioning those described in *Bhagavad Gita*.

Karma yoga

For active people Krishna offers karma yoga, the path of selfless action, which is described in detail in the Bhagavad Gita. Meaning both 'action' and 'effect', karma is any action performed by thought, word or deed, for which we are responsible. Karma is also our destiny, the luck we create for ourselves according to our actions. The law of karma is that of cause and effect: the principle that the consequences of our actions return to us inescapably, and eventually we have to balance the accounts. We find the same idea in other religions such as Christianity, summed up in the biblical saying,

The Indian political and spiritual leader Mahatma Gandhi was a supreme example of a karma yogi, working tirelessly to abolish the Hindu caste system and achieve social reform. He gave his life in pursuit of his ideals and died as a true *bhakta*, or devotee of God, with the name of God – *Ram* – on his lips.

'whatsoever a man soweth, that shall he also reap'. In Indian philosophies, such as Buddhism and yoga, karma is linked to the concept of reincarnation.

Karmic debts must be repaid, but so long as we do everything with a sense of attachment we continue to create more karma for ourselves, good or bad, and remain caught up in the wheel of life and death. The purpose of karma yoga is to become free of karma and liberated from the continuous cycle of reincarnation. This is done by relinquishing the sense of 'doership', although not the responsibility, and becoming the instrument through which actions are performed rather than their author. This corresponds with the Taoist concept of *wu-wei*, or inaction in action, and the sense of non-doership is reinforced through meditation. In hatha yoga the same concept finds expression in B.K.S. Iyengar's teaching that postures should be performed with 'effortless effort'. In karma yoga actions and their fruits are performed as an offering, in a spirit of self-surrender.

Karma yoga is a path that can be practised equally well by people living in the hurly-burly of everyday life and by those who have already renounced it. The key to this path is to act dispassionately, without attachment or expectation of reward. Karma yoga is wisdom in action and is usually combined with other forms of yoga.

This colourful 18th century Indian painting shows one of the most famous stories of the *Bhagavad Gita* in which Krishna single-handedly lifts Mount Govardhana to protect the villagers and their livestock from the wrath of the god Indra.

Jnana yoga

Truth is within ourselves; it takes no rise
From outward things, whate'er you may believe.
There is an inmost centre in us all,
Where truth abides in fullness; and around,
Wall upon wall, the gross flesh hems it in,
This perfect, clear perception – which is truth.
A baffling and perverting carnal mesh
Binds it, and makes all error: and, to know,
Rather consists in opening out a way
Whence the imprisoned splendour may escape,
Than in effecting entry for a light
Supposed to be without.   *Paracelsus*, Robert Browning

For those of a contemplative nature Krishna recommends jnana yoga, the path of knowledge and wisdom. The practices of jnana yoga are twofold. Intellectual knowledge of the truth is gained through study and the reading of scriptures, contemplation and reflection on the truths they impart. This anchors and purifies the mind, but is not in itself enough to lead to enlightenment. Buddha compared scholars content with knowledge gleaned from books and discourses to herdsmen of other men's cows. When theoretical understanding is balanced by meditation on the unity of all things, however, it eventually gives way to direct experience of the truth. It is this direct experiential knowledge of the true nature of reality that lies at the heart of jnana yoga.

The great Indian sage Ramana Maharshi, a modern jnana yogi, taught the ancient practice of self-enquiry as being the best path to enlightenment. According to Maharshi the enquiry 'Who am I? destroys all other thoughts and, finally, itself – 'just as a stick used for stirring the burning funeral pyre gets consumed'. When there is no trace left of the 'I'-thought, only the substratum of pure consciousness, the Self, which underlies all states of mind, remains.

Bhakti yoga

Bhakti yoga, the path of devotion and love for God, is the third of the great yogic paths described in the *Bhagavad Gita* and is placed by Krishna above all other forms of yoga. Devotees may worship God in unmanifest form, but more often in a personal form. The many divine personages of the Hindu pantheon – are all considered different manifestations of the one God.

Bhakti yoga is the closest yogic path to the practices of Christianity, Judaism and Islam, all of which have developed the concept of a personal God to whom acts of praise and worship are directed. Songs of praise feature in bhakti yoga, and it is often integrated with other forms of yoga, in particular karma yoga and mantra yoga – the chanting of God's name out loud or silently. Other practices may include meditation on the image of the chosen form of God.

The ultimate aim of bhakti yoga is to surrender to and ultimately merge with God through intense devotion, much as the Christian or Sufi mystic becomes one with the Beloved.

Do not become distracted by attempting to analyse Divine Mystery… A few sips of the precious wine of Love will thoroughly intoxicate you. Why leave the glass untouched on the table while inquiring how the wine was produced or estimating how many gallons may exist in the infinite wine cellar? Ramakrishna, 19th century Indian mystic

Be your own guide and your own torch.

Buddha

As in yoga, good posture is considered important for meditation. The classic pose is the lotus position
as shown by this Buddha in a 9th century Buddhist temple in Borabudur, Indonesia.

From the knowledge and insight borne of meditation arose one of the world's greatest spiritual traditions. According to Buddhism, Buddhas or 'awakened ones' have appeared throughout history, the historical Buddha being the latest in a long line that extends into the future. However, the various forms of Buddhism we know today are based on the teachings of Siddhartha Gautama, who became known as the Buddha after he attained enlightenment.

Several centuries elapsed between the Buddha's death and the recording of his life and teachings, but legend tells that Siddhartha Gautama was born of a noble family in Nepal around 563 BC. His

Buddhism

was a miraculous conception and birth duly heralded by portentous events. The future Buddha is said to have entered the womb of his mother, Maya, in the form of a white elephant with six tusks, through which he pierced his mother's side. Ten months later the infant Siddhartha was painlessly delivered from Maya's side, unstained and unpolluted, as she stood holding the branch of a tree. Unfortunately, Maya died seven days after giving birth to her son and he was raised by her sister, Mahaprajapati, who subsequently married the young Siddhartha's father, Shuddhodana.

Not long after the birth Shuddhodana received a visit from the sage Asita, who immediately recognized on the infant's tiny body the thirty-two marks that, according to prophecy, marked him out as a future Buddha. Shuddhodana was far from pleased to hear this, knowing that the life of an ascetic would mean the discontinuation of the family line, and made up his mind to shield his son from the harsher realities of life that might turn his mind towards religion and bring about the fulfilment of the prophecy.

As a result Siddhartha Gautama led a very sheltered, if privileged, life, cloistered away in a palace, but with every kind of pleasure and luxury at his disposal. At sixteen he was married but, restless and curious about the outside world, Siddhartha arranged on four fateful occasions to be driven out by his charioteer. The Four Meetings, as they are called, altered the course of Siddhartha's life. On the first occasion he encountered an old man, on the second a sick man, on the third a corpse about to be cremated. It was then, with a shock, that he realized for the first time that old age, sickness and death, and the misery and suffering that accompanies them, were the inescapable lot of man. Suddenly the pleasures of palace life began to pall.

Young Buddhist monks on the terrace of the Began temple complex in Burma. The colour of their robes is symbolic of the spiritual fire which burns away impurities.

On the fourth occasion, however, Siddhartha encountered a *sadhu*, or wandering monk. Penniless and dressed in rags, the monk nevertheless impressed Siddhartha with his bearing and aura of contentment and tranquillity. So struck was he by the monk and, in sharp contrast, the pictures of human suffering presented on the previous meetings, that Siddhartha concluded that mankind's salvation lay in abandoning worldly life and pursuing the Truth through various austerities and meditation. Now aged twenty-nine, he resolved to leave the palace, abandoning his wife and family (fortunately a son had been born to carry on the family line) and, vowing to save not only himself but the whole of humanity from the pain and misery inherent in life, he set out on a spiritual quest to find the answer to the problem of human suffering.

For six years Siddhartha sought the teachings of Brahmins, yogis and other holy men. He practised severe austerities, subjecting his body to extreme fasting, exposure to the elements, and much more. Eventually, in a state of emaciation and realizing that neither teachings nor ascetic practices had brought him closer to the knowledge he sought, Siddhartha accepted a bowl of food to give him strength. Then he fashioned a cushion out of grass and sat to meditate under the famous Bodhi Tree, a species of fig, at a site – now a place of pilgrimage – known today as Bodh Gaya, in the modern Indian state of Bihar. It was here, after being offered all manner of temptations by Satan and being psychically attacked by hordes of demons, that Siddhartha, henceforward known as the Buddha, finally attained full enlightenment and realized both the causes of and cure for all suffering. Thus, from Siddhartha's meditation under the Bodhi Tree Buddhism was born.

The Buddha's teachings

Having experienced the extremes of worldliness and asceticism, the Buddha realized the futility of both and taught the Middle Way, a path that lies between self-indulgence, which runs counter to spiritual progress, and self-mortification, which is mentally and physically damaging.

Not long after his enlightenment, the Buddha preached his first sermon at the deer park near Benares, setting out the doctrine of the Four Noble Truths that lie at the heart of all Buddhist teachings.

The Four Noble Truths

1   The truth that human life is transitory and involves suffering (*dukkha*). Dukkha is usually translated as 'suffering', but should be interpreted in the widest sense, ranging from mental anguish to extreme physical pain, total despair and desperation to the petty frustrations of life. The Buddha does not deny life's pleasures and happiness, but even these are tinged with sadness because we know they cannot last.

The Wheel of Life, a symbolic representation of the cycle of existence, is widespread in Tibetan Buddhism and illustrates different levels of existence: the realms of the gods, antigods and humans above; animals, ghosts and hell below. Common to all these is the experience of suffering and death, represented by Yama, the god of the underworld, who holds the wheel in his claws and spins it around.

2   The truth that suffering is caused by ignorance of our true nature, which brings about desire. On a gross level this may take the form of sexual desire, an unbridled lust for power or money, or craving for attention or fame. On a subtler level, even the wish to do good and make the world a better place, or to find more meaning in life, are still desires. Desire in its turn leads to the cycle of rebirth, powering the endless motion of the Wheel of Life.

3   The truth that there is a way to end the suffering brought about by desire and false beliefs. When desire and ignorance are cleared away we are liberated from the Wheel of Life and and experience *nirvana*, the ultimate freedom and the supreme goal of Buddhism.

4   The truth that we can become free from desire and ignorance by following the Middle Way. This is an eightfold path consisting of right understanding, right thought, right speech, right action, right livelihood, right effort, right mindfulness and right concentration.

Like yoga, Buddhism is more a way of liberation than a religion, offering an array of spiritual practices from moral precepts to a wide range of meditative practices. The Middle Way has parallels with the eight limbs of yoga, and the steps along it should be seen as complementary to one another rather than as a hierarchical ladder to be ascended rung by rung.

Buddhist meditation

The last two steps of the Middle Way deal specifically with meditation, which is central to Buddhism, bringing about insight and understanding of the true nature of reality, which cannot be gained through theoretical knowledge, and leading to lasting peace of mind and spiritual transformation.

The practice of concentration involves focussing on a single object, concept or process such as the breath, a coloured wheel, love, compassion or any attribute of the Buddha, or a physical sensation. Concentration prepares the meditator for *vipassana*, the path of insight, in which the mind is opened rather than narrowly focussed. This involves the practice of mindfulness, which directs attention to the present moment and all that enters into it. As a meditation technique, mindfulness begins by bringing awareness to the breath, then gradually extending it to your body, feelings, emotions and mind. You should adopt a neutral attitude to thoughts and feelings, being aware of them without comment. Mindfulness leads to progressively higher states of insight (*vipassana*) and transcendental experiences (*nirvana*), which are initially fleeting, but which are gradually maintained for longer periods.

In keeping with the principle of the Middle Way, the Buddha had a balanced approach to meditation and the mind. As the story about the Buddha and the sitar player on page 27 shows, the Buddha taught that in meditation the mind should not be constrained or permitted to roam, but allowed to settle naturally through the use of techniques such as those above.

A 19th century Tibetan thangka, or religious painting, showing Amitayus, the Buddha of Infinite Life, surrounded by numerous boddhisattvas and other divine beings. Thangkas are used as an aid in the practice of complex visualisations, a form of meditation common in Tibetan Buddhism.

The spread of Buddhism

The Buddha probably taught in an ad hoc fashion, adapting his teachings to individual needs and situations. Like most mystics he regarded intellectual speculation and learning as a distraction on the path to liberation and was not interested in expounding a new philosophy. Nevertheless, various schools of Buddhism emerged after his death, each with a different interpretation of the basic teachings or emphasizing different aspects.

The two main schools today are Theravada, believed by its followers to represent the Buddha's original teachings most closely, and Mahayana. The Theravada school, also known as the Hinayana ('Little Vehicle'), regards Buddha as an enlightened but human teacher who showed others a way to achieve his state, though few individuals are held to be capable of achieving this. The Mahayana ('Great Vehicle') school considers the Buddha to be the embodiment of absolute truth and holds that all have the potential to achieve enlightenment.

While the main meditation practice of Theravada Buddhism is mindfulness, Mahayana has developed a wide range of practices and techniques. The Vajrayana ('Diamond Vehicle') school, for example, commonly known as Tantric Buddhism, developed out of the Mahayana school and combines elements of yoga with Buddhist teachings. Initiation is central to this path, which shares many features with Tantric yoga (see pages 70–71) and embraces a number of esoteric approaches to meditation. Music and art are a strong feature of both Buddhist and yogic approaches to Tantra, which cultivates artistic experience both for its own sake and for the powerful emotions and passions it arouses. Through Tantric techniques, the energy released via such responses is harnessed to fuel the pursuit of spiritual knowledge.

Zen (see below), a highly distinctive form of Buddhism best known for its direct yet enigmatic methods and its use of *koans* (devices intended to cut through logical, conceptual ways of thinking and awaken to other levels of consciousness) is also a school of Mahayana Buddhism.

Buddhism declined in India, its country of origin, becoming more or less extinct by the thirteenth century BC, but from around the third century AD onwards it had begun to spread beyond the borders of its native land, adapting itself to local conditions and customs as it did so, and today is a major world religion. Theravada Buddhism is the dominant belief in Sri Lanka, Thailand, Burma and Cambodia; Mahayana is found in China, Japan, Vietnam and Korea; Vajrayana in Tibet, Mongolia and Japan. Because it is remarkably free from dogma, Buddhism finds expression equally in the simplicity of Theravada as in the colour and richness of Vajrayana, not to mention the creative originality of Zen. But although practised in different ways, all forms of Buddhism stress the importance of direct experience of spiritual truths over belief or blind faith, and all emphasize the central importance of meditation in achieving this.

If you walk, just walk. If you sit, just sit; but whatever you do, don't wobble.

Unmon, 10th century Chinese Zen master

Zen brush painting of a meditator by Shifu Nagaboshi Tomio.

Eating when hungry, sleeping when tired. This is Zen. But performing such simple acts of everyday life properly, with full attention, is no easy matter.

Zen is the form of Buddhism we are most familiar with. Over the last century it has taken root in the West, especially in America, and established a huge following, much as it did several centuries ago in China, where it was shaped by strong cultural influences, particularly Taoism, and subsequently in Japan, where it is as much a way of life as a way of enlightenment. Zen has exercised a huge influence on Japanese culture – without it there would be no *haiku* (a form of Japanese poetry) or tea ceremonies – and its contribution to art and design in the West is now also apparent. In both East and West, Zen has been a source of inspiration for creative arts from poetry and painting to architecture and gardening. 'Zen style' has a spontaneous, direct, fluid, harmonious, yet unexpected quality. This quality is embodied in the brush paintings so characteristic of Zen, their seeming simplicity stemming from a masterly use not only of the brush, but of form and space. Empty space is a striking feature of Zen paintings, gardens and architecture, yet this emptiness is an integral aspect of the whole, just as our original nature is empty of all thoughts of 'self' and 'other':

Z e n

> *Only when you have no thing in your mind and no mind in things*
> *are you vacant and spiritual, empty and marvellous.* Te-shan

Apart from its spiritual dimension, Zen's influence on Western culture can be seen in practical arts such as interior design and flower arrangement. The word 'Zen' has entered our language to describe a certain taste and aesthetic – loosely speaking minimalist, with a twist. Yet for all our easy familiarity with the language of Zen – and our use of the word is not completely inappropriate given that Zen sweeps aside all the paraphernalia of religious ritual and dogma, and focuses on the heart of the matter – the way of Zen remains elusive.

The old pond.
A frog jumps in.
Plop! Matsuo Basho, 17th century haiku master

Zen, the Japanese rendering of *ch'an*, which is in turn the Chinese version of the Sanskrit *dhyana* (see page 53), literally means meditation. As discussed above, meditation is the essence of all forms of Buddhism, but what really distinguishes Zen from other schools is its direct methods of pointing to the truth, in particular its unique use of *koans*. These are usually anecdotes or sayings of Zen masters, and take the form of problems that are insoluble through logical thinking. One of the best-known koans was created by the Zen master Hakuin, who clapped his hands, then raised one hand and asked, 'What is the sound of one hand?' By confounding rational thought processes koans can trigger a breakthrough in consciousness known as *satori* or awakening, a sudden flash of illumination that opens up a new way of looking at the world.

According to tradition, Zen originated in the sixth century AD with the arrival in China of Bodhidharma, an Indian Buddhist monk. A legendary exchange between the monk and the Chinese Emperor Wu, a devout Buddhist who had built several temples and done countless good deeds in the hopes of promoting the cause of Buddhism and securing for himself the best possible future lives, is characteristic of Zen. When the Emperor asked Bodhidharma what merit he had gained through his good deeds, the monk answered abruptly, 'No merit whatever.' (Do-gooding for the sake of future reward is abhorrent to Zen.) Asked about the supreme meaning of the sacred truth of Buddhism, Bodhidharma replied, 'Vast empti-

ness – nothing sacred.' The Emperor then demanded to know, 'Who is this that stands before us?' 'I don't know,' returned Bodhidharma, thus revealing the essence of his teaching.

The Emperor didn't grasp his meaning. Bodhidharma's direct approach found little favour with him and the monk withdrew from the court and retired to Shaolin Monastery in the adjacent state of Wei, where he spent the next nine years in a cell, meditating in front of a wall until a more suitable disciple turned up.

Bodhidharma is recognized as the first patriarch of Zen (or Ch'an) in China, but Zen Buddhists trace their lineage back to the Buddha in an unbroken line, beginning with Mahakashyapa, the first patriarch of the Indian lineage. His awakening is said to have been transmitted directly by the Buddha one day when, instead of giving a discourse to his assembled disciples, he merely held up a single lotus flower, remaining completely silent. With this gesture the truth suddenly struck Mahakashyapa, who quietly smiled. An answering smile from the Buddha acknowledged that the transmission had occurred. The story is considered to be the origin of Zen, symbolizing that the real message always remains unspoken, yet can be conveyed by 'direct pointing'.

Today the two main schools of Zen are Soto and Rinzai, both of which place great emphasis on *zazen* ('sitting meditation'), the cornerstones of which are posture, breathing and attitude. Unlike most forms of yogic meditation, which involve focussing attention on a chosen thought or object

such as a mantra or a candle, the practice of zazen, as the name suggests, involves simply sitting in a state of quiet awareness, doing nothing, without purpose or aim. Thoughts and images are allowed to come and go, floating through the mind like clouds in the sky, neither grasped at nor shut out. However, beginners are often advised to focus on their breathing, counting consecutive breaths from one to ten then starting over again. The ideal posture for meditation is considered to be the lotus position (page 130) or, if this is difficult, the half lotus (page 132), keeping the trunk upright and chin drawn in so that the tip of the nose is directly over the navel. The eyes are kept slightly open, looking down about one metre ahead, but without focussing. The hands are placed palms upward in the lap, left over right, with the tips of the thumbs touching. Correct breathing – deep, calm and rhythmic – follows naturally from correct posture. From these two flows the correct attitude of mind – opening out one's attention and being conscious of whatever is happening internally and externally, and simply letting it be without comment or interference.

Bodhidharma, the legendary founder of Zen, is traditionally portrayed as a fierce-looking character, glowering through bulbous, protruding eyes. One story tells how he was so enraged after falling asleep during meditation that he sliced off his eyelids to prevent it from happening again. At the exact spot where his eyelids fell, the first tea plant sprouted. Ever since then tea has been plentifully supplied to Zen monks to keep them awake and alert during long hours of meditation.

Sitting quietly, doing nothing, Spring comes, and the grass grows by itself

From the *Zenrin Kushu,* a collection of Zen sayings

In the Soto school, zazen is the main practice. Koans are also used, but not as a meditation technique. By contrast, the practice of Rinzai Zen revolves around the use of koans, which are given to the Zen student by his or her teacher and systematically worked on during meditation. Working with a koan is a completely non-intellectual exercise. Rather than trying to find a logical solution to the koan, the student aims to become one with it, embedding it within his or her consciousness. With the solving of the koan – which may or may not occur during meditation – comes *satori*, the goal of this form of Zen training.

Zen can only be truly understood through practical experience and training, but its essential nature is encapsulated in the following four statements attributed to its founder, Bodhidharma:

A special transmission outside the scriptures.

No dependence upon sacred writings.

Direct pointing to the human heart.

Seeing into one's nature and attaining Buddhahood.

The minimalist garden of Dai-sen at the Zen monastery at Daitoku-ji, Japan, has a powerful meditative quality. The carefully raked lines of white gravel draw the eye inwards, creating an impression of space and a calm and contemplative atmosphere.

Being and non-being create each other.

Difficult and easy support each other.

Long and short define each other.

High and low depend on each other.

Before and after follow each other.

Lao-tzu

A Sung dynasty statue of Lao-tzu riding a water buffalo.

Philosophical Taoism, as distinct from religious Taoism, which is more concerned with the pursuit of immortality and the acquisition of magical powers, is a mystical teaching best represented by the works of Lao-tzu ('the Old Master'), the legendary author of the *Tao Te Ching*, and Chuang-tzu, who, together with Lao-tzu, is considered one of the founders of philosophical Taoism.

Lao-tzu is traditionally said to have been a contemporary of Confucius, who lived in the sixth century BC, but scholars date the work attributed to him to the third or fourth century BC. Little is known of the life of Lao-tzu – or even if he actually existed – but according to popular legend he was Custodian of the Imperial Archives in the state of Chou, where he lived his life in accordance with the Tao and the Te (the Supreme Way and its Expression). The decline of the state prompted his departure from the court and he headed west, coming to a mountain pass where he was stopped by Yin-hsi, the Guardian of the Pass. Yin-hsi implored the sage to write a book for his enlightenment before passing through the gate, upon which Lao-tzu took out his pen and, in one sitting, composed the *Tao Te Ching* (the book of the Tao and the Te), consisting of five thousand pictograms. Handing it to Yin-hsi, Lao-tzu passed through the gate and went on his way, and was never heard of again.

Apocryphal or not, the story of the *Tao Te Ching*'s beginnings is in the spirit of the book itself, which points to the Way and opens the gate, bringing the seeker within sight of the goal of Taoism, which is to return to the Way.

Taoism

The highest virtue is not virtuous; therefore it truly has virtue. The lowest virtue never loses sight of its virtue; therefore it has no true virtue.   Lao-tzu

The Tao and the Te

The tao that can be told
is not the eternal Tao.
The name that can be named
is not the eternal Name.

The unnameable is the eternally real.
Naming is the origin
of all particular things.

Lao-tzu

The starting point for understanding Taoist philosophy is to understand what is meant by the Tao. Tao translates literally as 'Way', but as the first lines (above) of the *Tao Te Ching* establish, the Tao is beyond description, and Lao-tzu later points out that he only calls it the 'Way' because he has to refer to it somehow. Tao is Lao-tzu's term for the Absolute or Ultimate Reality, in its transcendent, undifferentiated, formless, impersonal, attributeless aspect. It is the substratum of existence, the primordial soup from which the physical universe manifests.

Te is usually translated as 'virtue', in the sense of inherent power or capacity, rather than simply in the sense of morality. Te is the natural expression of Tao as it manifests in the physical world: the creative force or life energy in things and their innate capacity to align themselves with the Way, unfolding in accordance with their own nature. Thus a wild flower naturally

blossoms and birds migrate at the appropriate time without any kind of self-awareness. For the Taoist, true virtue arises when we move along the course natural or proper to us, rather than against the regular flow of things, and is entirely unconcerned with conforming to conventionally approved codes of conduct and morality. Those who are genuinely virtuous spontaneously say and do the right thing without their even being aware of it, and with no thought of reward or approval.

Returning to the Tao

While other creatures and species follow the natural flow, man, through his habit of analyzing situations, weighing up the pros and cons and choosing between the alternatives, has lost the ability to act spontaneously and genuinely, and has departed from the Way. Because we have lost touch with who we truly are by our very nature, we constantly strive to be something we are not. From this stem all man's problems, both individually and collectively as a society. The goal of Taoism, then, is to return to the Way.

Of central importance in returning to the Way is the Taoist concept of *wu-wei* ('non-action' or 'without action'). This does not mean that Taoism advocates literally doing nothing or being passive. Nor does it imply withdrawing from the hurly-burly of life. What wu-wei really denotes is a form of action that is entirely unpremeditated and without motive or intention, yet invariably effective and appropriate to the situation. Wu-wei is the spontaneous action of one who moves in accord with the Tao.

> *Those who have heard the Tao decrease day after day.*
> *They decrease and decrease till they get to the point*
> *where they do nothing.*
> *They do nothing and yet there's nothing left undone.*

Lao-tzu

The individual who acts in accord with the Way is attentive to every situation and what it calls for, unerringly responding with the right action, like a master craftsman practising his or her art. This spontaneous way of acting, intervening only as and when needed, is beyond the reach of those who habitually apply rules and reason, deliberating on the best possible course of action before proceeding. This is illustrated by Chuang-tzu with the story of a swimmer who was spotted by Confucius in a whirlpool. Asked how he stayed afloat, the swimmer replied:

> *'I enter with the inflow, and emerge with the outflow, fol-*
> *low the Way of the water and do not impose my selfishness*
> *upon it. This is how I stay afloat in it... Having been born*
> *on dry land I am at home on dry land – it's native to me.*
> *Having grown up in water I am at home in water – it's*
> *natural to me. It is so without me knowing why it is so –*
> *it's destined for me.'*

Many great artists have described a certain quality of 'non-authorship' in relation to their work – the sensation of their art flowing through them and emerging of its own accord rather than being imposed or directed by them. 'We do not compose,' wrote Gustav Mahler (1860–1911) in connection with his Third Symphony, 'we are composed.' In a similar vein the visionary poet and painter William Blake (1757–1827) said that he wrote only, 'when commanded by the spirits, and the moment I have written, I see the words fly about the room in all directions'.

How does the Taoist return to the Way?

Empty your mind of all thoughts.

let your heart be at peace.

Watch the turmoil of beings,

but contemplate their return.

Each separate being in the universe

returns to the common source.

Returning to the source is serenity.

Lao-tzu

Both Lao-tzu and Chuang-tzu point to meditation practices as the way to become one with the Tao and experience mystically its emptiness, and the unity of all things within it. Although neither gives explicit techniques of meditation, many passages, such as that above, allude to traditional methods of stilling the mind. The importance given to *wu-wei* (non-action) suggests early Taoists may have practised a form of meditation closely resembling the Zen method of zazen. Chuang-tzu describes a practice called 'fasting the mind', also involving focussing the attention and emptying the mind of thoughts and perceptions:

Make your will one! Don't listen with your ears, listen with your mind. No, don't listen with your mind, but listen with your spirit. Listening stops with the ears, the mind stops with recognition, but spirit is empty and waits on all things. The Way gathers in emptiness alone. Emptiness is the fasting of the mind.

Breath awareness and various forms of controlled breathing, which typically involve guiding the *chi* (the life force, which manifests externally as the breath) through the body in ways not dissimilar to those of kundalini yoga, play an important role in Taoist meditation, not simply as a means to mystical insight, but also as a way to health and longevity. Taoists also practise several forms of moving meditation such as *t'ai chi chu'an*, which is characterized by soft flowing movements co-ordinated with breathing, aimed at turning the mind inward and realigning the mind and body with the Tao.

Tai chi practitioners performing their movements in the calm environment of the Temple of Heaven in Beijing.

The yin-yang symbol

Within the Tao, the supreme reality which pervades all existence, are two polarities, yin and yang. Yin, the feminine principle, is passive, receptive, dark and soft, while yang is masculine, active, creative, light and hard. The intermingling of these complementary principles gives rise to the phenomenal world in a cycle of coming into being and then ebbing away as all things eventually transform into their opposite – night into day, hot into cold. Yin and yang are intrinsic to one another, like the two sides of a coin, each having existence only by virtue of the other.

The yin-yang symbol expresses the creation of the universe. The circle represents ultimate reality and is divided into yin (usually shown as a dark shape) and yang (usually shown as a light shape), which underlie the world of forms and objects. Within each shape is a spot of the opposite colour, indicating that each opposing force holds the seed of its opposite, and will transform into it. This interaction of yin and yang gives rise to a state of continual change and transition – the movement of the Tao – and the balance between these energies governs the health and wellbeing of all things.

This stone yin-yang symbol, surrounded by signs of the Chinese zodiac, can be seen in the grounds of a temple in Chengdu, in the Sichuan Province of China.

Kindle in thy heart the flame of love,
And burn utterly thoughts and fine expressions.

Jalaluddin Rumi

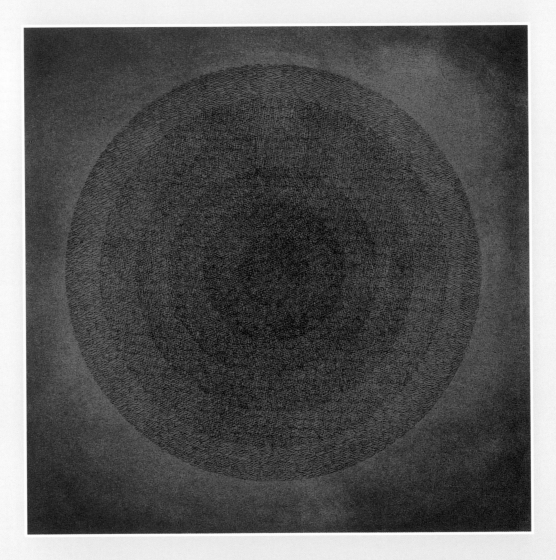

Round Dance, 1992, by Shirazeh Houshiary, was inspired by the poetry of the Sufi mystic

Jalaluddin Rumi, and expresses man's journey towards wholeness. The centre symbolizes

the still point of spiritual purity around which all existence moves.

Sufism is a mystical path associated with Islam that teaches the way to truth through divine love. Many Sufi teachers trace their lineage directly back to Mohammed, the Prophet whose revelations form the basis of Islam. However, the origins of Sufism are uncertain. Orthodox Sufis hold firmly to the Koran, the sacred text comprising the revelations of the Prophet, and insist that there can be no Sufism outside of Islam. Other Sufi scholars believe that Sufism arose in the 9th century BC as a reaction to the theology and legal system that the Koranic teachings gave rise to. Yet others are unconcerned with religion or the lack of it, holding that

Sufism

Sufism is the essence of all religions, that it has always existed, and that it predates Islam. In practice the large majority of Sufis today are Muslim, many of them living in India where Sufism has a wide following. In the West, Sufism has also attracted a strong following but its practice does not generally involve embracing Islam.

The goal of Sufism is the complete evolution and refinement of man, and the transcending of everyday consciousness to penetrate the reality that lies beyond the normal boundaries of thought and the senses. Initiation, and the relationship between a Sufi master and his students, is central to Sufism, but the training procedures through which spiritual developent occurs are extremely diverse, to the point where different Sufi orders appear to have little in common with one another. Sufis acknowledge this, maintaining that it is only by continuously evolving and adapting outwardly that the inner teaching – the timeless and unchanging essence of Sufism – can be transmitted. Rather than setting up institutionalized ways of operating and handing out standard prescriptions for spiritual development, Sufis teach in response to particular needs at particular times, continually imparting their knowledge in fresh ways. Sufi training may involve storytelling, music, dancing, meditation, chanting, silence, particular tasks, various kinds of therapy, the practice of art forms such as calligraphy, or any combination of these.

Underlying the rich diversity of all these practices is the alchemical power of love to transform human consciousness. The Sufi path is devotional in character, and love of God – the losing of oneself in God – lies at the heart of the Sufi way.

What the eyes see is knowledge.
What the heart knows is Certainty.

Dhun'nun, 9th century Egyptian mystic

An important practice within many Sufi orders is *dhikr*, the remembrance of God through recitation of the Divine name or sacred passages from the *Koran*. These may be chanted in a group or used for solitary meditation, when they are repeated silently like a mantra with intense devotion and concentration. Like yogis, Sufis hold that certain sounds resonate with aspects of the Divine, and through repeating them an individual is imbued with divine consciousness and eventually attains mystical knowledge of God. Unlike some other mystical traditions, the Sufi conception of God is a personal one and Sufis are careful to maintain a distinction between man and God. However, the boundaries can become blurred, a notorious example being that of Mansur Mastana, who cried out in a state of mystical ecstasy, 'I am God, I am God.' The authorities did not understand and hanged him for heresy. Mansur has been revered as a Sufi saint ever since.

Even so, many Sufis find the idea of union with God inconsistent with the Koranic teachings, if not utterly blasphemous. A more acceptable mystical goal is expressed in the doctrine of the 'Perfect Man', also known as 'Universal Man'. Perfect Man was created by God in his own image and is a kind of intermediary between man and God. Rather than uniting with God, the Sufi attains mystical union with Perfect Man. Once established in the truth, the Sufi lives 'in the world but not of it', doing the will of God.

Besides *dhikr*, Sufis employ many other forms of meditation such as visualization and, famously, the unique meditational dance form of the Whirling Dervishes of the Mavlevi Order, established by the celebrated mystic, poet and Sufi master Jalaluddin Rumi. The dance is a sacred ritual in which the dervishes, clad in traditional costume of dark brimless caps and long white robes with wide skirts, are transported into a state of divine intoxication. To the musical accompaniment of a reed pipe, along with drums and chanting, the dervishes spin round and round, faster and faster, making symbolic gestures with their hands, head and arms. Losing all sense of self, the dervish is transformed into God's instrument, receiving blessings with the right palm, which is extended upwards towards heaven, and dispensing them earthwards with the left. As Divine grace flows through him or her, the dervish becomes one with the Beloved.

I believe in the religion
Of love
Whatever directions its caravan
    may take,
For love is my religion and my
    faith.

Ibn al-'Arabi, 13th century Andalusian mystic

The Beloved

One went to the door of the Beloved and
knocked. A voice asked, 'Who is there?'
He answered, 'It is I.'
The voice said, 'There is no room here for me
and thee.' The door was shut.
After a year of solitude and deprivation this man
returned to the door of the Beloved.
He knocked.
A voice from within asked, 'Who is there?'
The man said, 'It is Thou.'
The door was opened for him.

Jalaluddin Rumi

16th century miniature depicting whirling dervishes
performing their dances.

If I am and You are because I am myself and You are Yourself,
then I am I and You are You. But if I am because
You are, I am not I and You are not You.

Rebbe Nachman

Illustration of the seven-branched candelabrum, or *Menorah*, from a 13th

century illuminated Hebrew manuscript.

The Jewish mystical tradition dates back to early times, possibly originating with the teachings of Moses, or perhaps to the esoteric teachings of the Essenes around the time of Christ. By far the most important movement within its history, however, is that of the Kabbalah – a Hebrew word meaning 'that which is received'. The teachings of the Kabbalah have had a chequered history, falling into disrepute in the seventeenth century and then again in the nineteenth. Nevertheless, the Kabbalistic heritage has had a profound impact on the development of modern Judaism and has played a major role within the Western esoteric tradition. Recently the Kabbalah has attracted renewed attention, fuelled by a number of celebrity devotees. In its more popular form the Kabbalah presents an accessible approach to spirituality that can be practised both by Jews and non-Jews, although some feel that its latest incarnation has little connection to traditional Jewish mysticism.

Kabbalah

Although rooted in earlier traditions, classical Kabbalah arose in the thirteenth century in Southern France and spread to Spain, where it was further developed by medieval Spanish Jews into a highly complex system of mysticism. Its main teachings are found in the *Zohar*, or *Book of Splendour*, written by the twelfth-century Spanish Kabbalist Moses de Leon, but traditionally ascribed to the second-century sage Rabbi Simeon bar Yohai. According to legend, Rabbi Simeon hid in a cave with his son to escape persecution by the Roman emperor Trajan. Following the death of the Emperor thirteen years later they emerged from hiding, but, troubled by the spiritual poverty he found amongst the Jews, Rabbi Simeon returned to his cave, intending to spend the rest of his life in meditation. After a year in solitary contemplation, he heard a voice telling him to go out and teach those who were ripe for his message. His teachings were recorded, by his followers, in the *Zohar*.

A 17th century roll depicting the Tree of Life, a central focus of Kabbalistic meditation representing the creation of the world. It is composed of ten sephiroth, or attributes of God, linked by twenty-two paths. During meditation involving visualization of the sephiroth, the Kabbalist ascends the Tree and achieves mystical communion with the Divine.

The *Zohar* distinguishes two aspects of God: *En Sof* (the 'Infinite'), eternally hidden and unknowable; and the manifest God revealed in mystical states, through whom the material world comes into being. According to Kabbalistic teachings, creation begins with the emanation of the *sephiroth*, or divine attributes, which are represented in the Tree of Life. Sometimes four Trees are depicted, one on top of the other, in the form of a Jacob's Ladder, to represent the Kabbalistic belief that the cosmos comprises four worlds: the world of the Divine, the world of Creation, the world of formation, and the world of the material and of action. These can also be understood as the eternal, spiritual, psychological and physical realms.

The paths that link the sephiroth signify the twenty-two letters of the Hebrew alphabet and their sounds, each being an aspect of the creative energy of the Divine. Together, the spheres and paths present a solid geometrical shape arranged in three columns, the two outer columns representing masculine and feminine, active and passive forces, and the central column representing the middle way, the balance between opposing forces, and the easiest and most direct path to God. On one level the Tree represents the universe, its roots going deep into the earth and its branches reaching up to heaven, and symbolizes the connection between them. On another level it represents man, the lower sephiroth corresponding to centres of the physical body, rather like the chakras of yoga, and the top three representing levels of knowledge or consciousness. Each sephira represents a stage in the creative process and a step in the attainment of wisdom, and each is associated with a rich and complex symbolism. Through meditation techniques similar to those used by yogis visualizing the chakras, the Kabbalist climbs the branches and attains mystical realization of divine unity – the goal of Kabbalistic teaching.

Another classic Kabbalistic technique that parallels certain yoga practices is meditation on the letters of the Hebrew alphabet, each of which is imbued with divine power. By concentrating on and permeating their consciousness with various combinations and permutations of these sacred letters, Kabbalists enter higher levels of consciousness. The practice dates back to medieval Spain, but was developed and given new impetus in the sixteenth century by the teacher Isaac Luria. Under his influence, the Kabbalah, which until then had been a secret teaching confined to a small minority of Jews, became a dominant force in Judaism.

During the eighteenth century the wisdom of the Kabbalah spread through the Hasidic movement that emerged from Luria's teachings, and still flourishes. This movement was led by mystic Israel ben Eliezer, called the Baal Shem Tov (the Master of the Holy Name). Unlike traditional Kabbalists, the Baal Shem Tov taught an ecstatic path of devotion to God – the practice of seeing God in everything and constant recitation of the names of God as the way to reach mystical awareness.

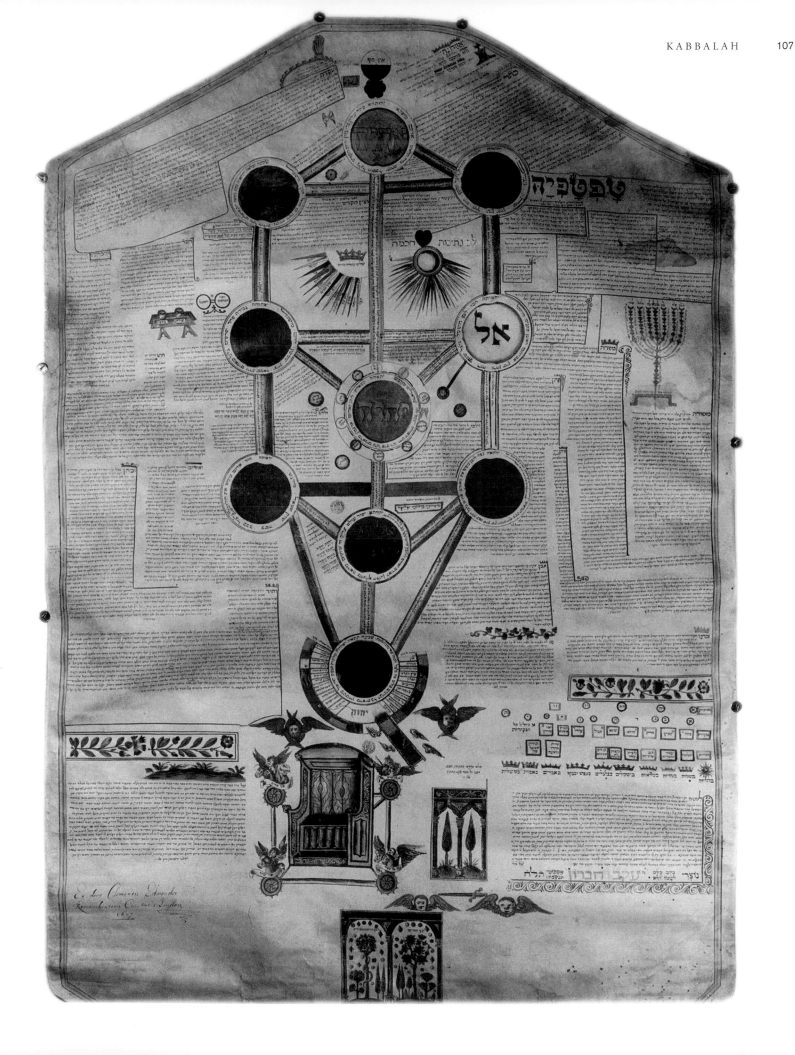

Be still, and know that I am God.

Psalms, 46:10

The Annunciation, one of the many frescoes depicting scenes from the
life of Christ and the Virgin painted by Fra Angelico in individual friars'
cells at San Marco, Florence, as an aid to devotion and contemplation.

Christianity, the dominant religion of the West, is based on the life and teachings of Jesus of Nazareth, whom Christians proclaim as the Son of God. The founding belief of Christianity is that Christ arose from the dead, an article of faith that has a broad history of interpretation, but that is accepted literally by many Christians as a physical return to the flesh. As in other religions, differences in doctrine and practice have resulted in the growth of separate denominations, the major divisions within the Church being Roman Catholicism, Eastern Orthodoxy and Protestantism. Although they offer different emphases and approaches to

Christian mysticism

worship, the main teachings of Christianity – belief in an omnipotent God, Jesus Christ as intermediary between man and God, the Passion and Resurrection of Christ, the Holy Trinity or union of the Father, Son and Holy Spirit in one Godhead – form the common basis of Christian belief.

Most people are familiar with Christian teachings, but its mystical element is sometimes overlooked. Mainstream Western Christianity tends to be associated more with morality and petitionary prayer – seeking help and healing for oneself or others – than with the silent communion with God found in contemplative prayer. Yet Christian mysticism has a long and venerable history, as evidenced from the influential mystical treatises attributed to Dionysius the Areopagite, St Paul's first convert in Athens, through to the spiritual writings of the twentieth-century Trappist monk Thomas Merton. Christian mystics whose teachings form the basis of meditation in Christian circles today include Julian of Norwich, a fourteenth-century English recluse, whose *Revelations of Divine Love* is an account of her mystical experiences. Many churches today have Julian groups, where people come together to meditate silently. *The Imitation of Christ*, a collection of prayers and maxims espousing a life of meditation and devotion to God, compiled by the fifteenth-century German mystic Thomas à Kempis is to this day read on a daily basis by many Christian groups and individuals as an inspiration for contemplation. The *Spiritual Exercises* written in the sixteenth century by Ignatius of Loyola still form the basis for Jesuit training, while his Spanish compatriots – and near contemporaries – Teresa of Avila and St John of the Cross are amongst the best-known and best-loved of Christian contemplative saints. In his writings St John described the suffering – a necessary process of spiritual purification – that accompanies the mystical journey towards God as the 'dark night of the soul', a phrase that has become synonymous with intense spiritual struggle.

The most godlike knowledge of God is that which
is known by unknowing.   St Dionysius

In essence, Christianity is a mystical religion – the way to God through union with Jesus Christ, the 'Word made flesh'. Christians believe that through his death on the cross Jesus took on the sins of the world and thereby absolved the world. Christians are baptized into Christ's death and resurrection and through this sacrament become members of the mystical body of Christ and are united in one spirit with God. This belief is renewed in the celebration of the Eucharist, or Holy Communion, when Christians partake of the consecrated bread and wine representing the body and blood of Jesus Christ. Christ's resurrection three days after his death symbolizes the spiritual rebirth and union with Christ that all can attain through his grace.

The deeper meaning of the cross and the resurrection, which lie at the heart of Christian mysticism, can only be truly understood through the religious experiences that silent contemplation fosters. There have always been contemplatives who have pondered these mysteries and those who practised the art of pure prayer – simply *being with* God rather than *thinking about* God, but within contemporary Christianity they form a minority. There are signs that the tide is turning, however, as more Christians turn to the silent prayer and recover the meditative practices of the early Christians.

The gospel of St Luke records how some Pharisees asked Jesus when the kingdom of God would come. He answered, 'The kingdom of God cometh not with observation: Neither shall they say, Lo here! or, lo there! for, behold, the kingdom of God is within you.' (*Luke 17:20–21*) In other words, the kingdom of God cannot be thought of in literal terms as a specific location up in the sky or anywhere else, nor will it 'arrive' at some time in the future. The kingdom of God is the knowledge of God within you, the mystical realization of union with Christ – and God – in the very here and now. The aim of Christian meditation, then, is to open oneself up and become receptive to the presence of God within, through stilling the mind while remaining alert and attentive. Although its focus is centred on Christ and his teachings, many of the techniques used in Christian meditation are universal.

The Desert Fathers, the early monks who inhabited the Egyptian desert, taught a method of meditation similar to the yogic technique of using a mantra, involving concentration, controlled breathing and a chosen biblical phrase or prayer. They also gave instructions concerning posture, recommending sitting with the body held upright but relaxed, with attention focussed towards the heart. Diodochus, the fifth century bishop of Photice, taught a way of reciting the 'Jesus' prayer silently in conjunction with the breath: 'Jesus Christ, Son of God' while breathing in, 'have mercy upon us' while breathing out. The prayer is best repeated – or simply 'heard' – slowly

This 19th century Russian icon entitled *The All-seeing Eye of God* draws the eye inwards, and could be used as a focus for visual meditation.

In the beginning was the Word, and the Word was with God, and the Word was God.   St. John

and rhythmically, over and over again like a mantra. Nothing else is needed – no concepts, images or thoughts, not even holy thoughts. Simply immerse your inner being in the energy of the prayer, and when your attention wanders, as it inevitably will, gently bring it back again. Any prayer can be used. The Lord's prayer ('Our Father which art in heaven, Hallowed be thy name...'), which Jesus taught his disciples (*Matthew 6:9–13*), adapts well to the natural rhythm of the breath and makes another good choice. An alternative is the Aramaic phrase *maranatha*, meaning 'Come, Lord'. An invocation to Christ, it was used in prayer by the first Christians, whose form of worship became known as the Way. It is found in St Paul's letter to the Corinthians (*I Corinthians 16:22*) and is a traditional choice for Christian meditation that can be repeated on both inhalation and exhalation. The popular Catholic practice of saying the rosary, a prayer devoted to the Virgin Mary, is similarly meditative, consisting of the recitation of fifty (or one hundred and fifty) *Ave Marias* and five (or fifteen) *Paternosters* (the Lord's prayer) and *Glorias* while meditating on specific Christian themes.

For centuries the Church was the greatest patron of the arts in Europe and it is no coincidence that in Western art galleries there are so many paintings depicting religious themes and events in the life of Christ and the saints. Christian mysteries such as the Annunciation, the Crucifixion and the Last Judgement have provided a source of inspiration for artists through the ages and many of these paintings were

originally intended as aids for contemplation and meditation, and were themselves painted as a spiritual exercise. In the Eastern Church icons provide a visual focus for meditation. These are consecrated representations of Christ, the Virgin Mary or the saints, usually painted in oil on wooden panels in traditional Byzantine style. Rather than portraying events in the Christian story, they are intended to convey a mystical experience and express the silence and mystery of God. As a focus for visual meditation they are typically contemplated by first gazing at them for a while, then closing the eyes and internalizing the image.

For many people music is the most sublime and direct of all art forms, elevating the spirit into the realms of transcendence. Within the Church, music has always played a major role in the form of psalms, hymns, plainsong and, of course, the great musical masterpieces, inspired by deep faith, of composers such as Bach (1685–1750). His *St Matthew's Passion* and *St John's Passion* were composed for the climax of the Church's year, a musical meditation on the events of Easter. For many who fail to find it in prayer, the aesthetic response to music has inspired a sense of mystical union and devotion to God.

At the very heart of the Christian mystical tradition lies the transformative power of love. It is only through love that the 'cloud of unknowing' that separates us from God can be penetrated. More important than the form any contemplative practice takes is the spirit in which it is carried out. This is true of all forms of meditation.

This 15th century painting by Giovanni Bellini, *St Francis in Ecstasy*,

shows the famous Christian rising to greet the morning sun.

THE PRACTICAL ART
of MEDITATION

3

The art of meditation is the art of shifting the focus of attention to ever subtler levels, without losing one's grip on the levels left behind.

I Am That, Nisargadatta Maharaj

Learning to meditate is possibly the best present you could ever give yourself, a way to delve beyond the surface layers of consciousness to the clarity and stillness of subtler levels of awareness. In the process, meditation takes you on an individual journey of self-discovery, giving you new insight into the workings of your mind and at times providing astonishing and quite extraordinary experiences.

The rewards of meditating are far reaching, yet in itself meditation is not a complicated business. Simple techniques often prove the most effective and allow meditation to arise easily, naturally and enjoyably. The more you enjoy it, the more likely you are to persevere, for, like any other skill – playing the piano, dancing or fencing – learning meditation takes time, practice, intelligence and dedication. The more you put into it, the more you are likely to gain from it. But unlike most skills, no special talents are needed other than a willingness to open your mind and give it a try. The rest will follow on from there. With interest and enthusiasm anyone can learn to meditate effectively.

This section outlines the basic principles and practice of meditation, and offers a selection – by no means exhaustive – of techniques you can experiment with in the comfort of your own home without adopting any philosophical or religious beliefs. Even if you can spare no more than ten minutes a day, by incorporating meditation into your life you will be making a positive contribution to your overall health and wellbeing – physical, mental, emotional and, of course, spiritual.

I know but one freedom and that is the freedom of the mind.

Antoine de St. Exupéry

The sculptor Constantin Brancusi's quest to reveal the innermost essence of things finds

expression in the simple elegance of his marble *Sleeping Muse III* (c. 1917).

The goal of meditation and mystical striving is a state of complete inner stillness in which no thoughts or images arise. Few people can achieve this without considerable practice, which is why meditation teachers devote so much attention to the issue of how to deal with the mind. In fact, Patanjali's famous definition of yoga states simply that it is the stilling of the movements of the mind. Meditation is the means to achieve this.

Most newcomers to meditation quickly discover the industrial capacity of the mind to churn out

Befriending your mind

thoughts in rapid succession onto the conveyor belt of consciousness, and just how wildly the mind can behave when they try to control it even for a few moments. Instead of slipping into a cosmic state of complete inner stillness they find themselves chasing minds that can race at quite breathtaking speed – dashing from London to Frankfurt and back in the space of about five seconds, having wined, dined, attended a few parties and done a few deals in the meantime. And that's on a good day! The capacity of the mind for non-stop busyness and activity is truly phenomenal, yet it is often when surface thoughts subside that the real heavy hitters come up – the memories of conflict and the deep-seated anxieties, the replayed conversations, the cravings and the emotions, the feelings of anger or worthlessness. And the more you try to banish them from your consciousness, the more insistently they enforce their presence.

No. 37 (Red), c.1956, by Mark Rothko. Rothko was committed to the expression of the spiritual through art, and believed that abstract form and pure colour had meaning only insofar as they represented higher truth.

There are many approaches to dealing with all the infinite scenarios that the mind conjures up during meditation, but attempting to expel them by force rarely works, as the meditation teacher Swami Muktananda liked to illustrate with the story of an earnest seeker who found himself plagued by the image of a monkey whenever he tried to meditate.

The story tells how the seeker went to a guru of great repute to ask for instruction in meditation and begged the guru for initiation. The guru agreed and at the auspicious moment the ritual was enacted. When all the formalities had been observed, the guru whispered a sacred and power-charged mantra into the ear of his new disciple with the appropriate instructions, adding the warning that he should never, ever, think of a monkey.

Although he thought it rather odd, the young man did not envisage any problems with this curious instruction since he never even gave monkeys a second thought. He went home, spread out his mat, bowed in all four directions in accordance with the guru's instructions, and sat to meditate. Of course the moment he closed his eyes the first thing that came into his head was the image of a black monkey. Horrified at his own unwitting disobedience to the guru's word, the disciple did his utmost to clear his mind of this apparition, but no matter what he did, every time he closed his eyes the image came back. In despair, the disciple returned to the guru who, having given his student an object lesson in how not to deal with the mind, set him up with another.

The truth is that meditation itself teaches you meditation, but having a few principles pointed out can save you from a lot of unnecessary mental meandering. One of the cardinal principles of meditation is to let the mind be, allowing thoughts and images to arise and subside without trying to subdue them and without getting caught up in them. This is easier said than done, of course, so if you find them very distracting, you could try one of the following approaches:

● Simply witness the different thoughts and images, desires and feelings that arise during meditation, without comment or judgement. Watch them pass through the sky of your mind like clouds floating by.

● With the understanding that your thoughts are nothing more than a manifestation of consciousness, allow them to dissolve back into the infinite expanse of consciousness, just like a raindrop falling into a lake merges with it.

● Think of your mind as a screen onto which a succession of images is projected. Try to discover who or what is projecting them, and who is watching them.

● Without trying to shut out thoughts or feelings, bring your awareness to the breath, a mantra or whatever focus you have chosen. This is the easiest method for many people and one of the reasons why techniques of meditation exist.

The techniques of meditation are employed to help us go beyond the surface chatter and busyness of the mind to the stillness deep within us. Once you enter that state of pure awareness there is no more need of them.

Smaller than the small, greater than the great,
the self is set in the heart of every creature. The
unstriving man beholds it, freed from sorrow.
Through tranquillity of the mind and the senses
he sees the greatness of the self.

Katha Upanishad

Spiritual transformation comes in its own time and cannot be hurried, any more

than you can speed up the development of an acorn into an oak tree.

Western culture is goal-oriented. It is interested in ends rather than means, and many people approach meditation in the same spirit, hankering after results and signs of achievement. But meditation is the opposite of this. Although it is helpful to clarify your goals at the outset, and to re-evaluate them from time to time, goals should be set aside during the actual period of practice. Meditation comes much more easily to those who do not seek and strive for results.

Nevertheless, how you measure progress in meditation depends largely on what you want from it. If

Signs of progress

your goal is to switch off and relax after a frazzled day at the office, or to recharge your batteries, or to awaken your innate powers of creativity, your success in achieving these ends is the benchmark by which success can be measured. As a bonus you will probably benefit in other ways, too. If your goals are more ambitious – and the ultimate aim of meditation is not to become anything, but to realize who and what you really are – then things may not always be quite so clear.

To some extent the quality of your meditation will tell you how much headway you are making. In the early stages the benefits are often felt mainly on a physical level – a feeling of general wellbeing and deep relaxation. As meditation deepens, the effects become more subtle as it begins to affect the psyche. Different feelings and emotions, both positive and negative, may arise and you may find yourself going through difficult periods. If these are unrelated to external things going on in your life, it could be that meditation has triggered a process of purification and you are feeling the effects. One of the things that can happen through meditation is that outworn thoughts and emotions blocking the flow of inner energy are brought to the surface of consciousness before being expelled. Just as the purification of the body that takes place when you fast or give up caffeine can make you feel worse (as toxins are released from the body) before you feel better, so with meditation. The release of physical, mental and emotional toxins can be uncomfortable, but it opens up the subtle pathways in the body and paves the way for greater inner freedom. Understand it as progress and treat negative experiences just as you do any thoughts and feelings that arise in meditation – simply witnessing them, and recognizing them as nothing other than phantasmagoria of consciousness.

After you have been meditating for a while your practice can lose its freshness and start to feel stale. You may feel you have reached a plateau, or even that you are losing ground. If so, it may help to experiment a bit – change your routine or approach to meditation, play around. Bear in mind that the journey of meditation is not a linear progression from one level to the next in orderly sequence. It is like a relationship or a marriage, with all the classic ups and downs. You fall in love – the flash of illumination – and go on honeymoon, experiencing the high of instantaneous meditation and profound experiences. After a while the excitement wears off and the familiarity of it all creates boredom. You go through an unsettled period. You feel little connection, nothing seems to be there. So you begin to question the relationship and perhaps even break it off, temporarily anyway. Then, realizing what you are missing, you renew your commitment. Often this is when the real work begins. The moral is, be patient, bearing in mind that inner evolution does not happen overnight. Illumination may come in a flash, like a thunderbolt, as with Saint Paul's vision on the road to Damascus, but it rarely comes unsought or without preparation. You have to put in the groundwork. All great sages agree that perseverance is always rewarded, but invariably it is when you least expect it. Just as you cannot speed up the process of an acorn growing into an oak tree, neither can you hurry your own development, spiritual or otherwise. With meditation you sow the seed and through perseverance – making time on a daily basis to just sit and be with your self in meditation – you prepare the soil and water it. Results come in their own time.

As you continue on your journey of meditation you may have experiences of various kinds. For example, you may feel rushes of energy circulating through your body or get tingling sensations. Involuntary physical movements may occur, such as your body swaying or shaking from side to side, symbolic hand gestures or even hatha yoga postures. You may notice changes in your breathing patterns, with the breath being spontaneously retained, forcibly expelled or the breathing becoming very shallow. Feelings of bliss and psychic phenomena, such as visions, inner lights and sounds, are not uncommon, especially in those who have had their inner energy awakened through initiation or their own efforts. These can encourage you in your practice and serve as a signpost that you are on track. However, clinging on to such phenomena and growing attached to them hinders further progress. They are best treated in much the same way as the images, emotions and desires that arise in meditation.

Fascinating as meditation experiences can be, real progress cannot be measured by whether or not you are on the receiving end of spectacular inner pyrotechnical displays or visionary experiences, or the magnificence and frequency of them. The ultimate experience has neither shape nor form, and no proof is needed. Real signs of spiritual attainment are a growing freedom from the anxieties and neuroses that can create so much unnecessary suffering, greater strength and an increased ability to handle any situation, a feeling of being more centred in your self, and a sense of deep inner calm. Above all, genuine spiritual development leads to greater love, kindness and compassion.

An ounce of practice is worth ten tons of theory

Swami Vishnu Devananda

The Shwe Dagon Pagoda, in Yangon, Burma, offers

a tranquil environment for meditation.

Iron discipline is not necessary for meditation, but it helps enormously to establish a routine, especially if you are new to it, and to develop good habits of posture and breathing from the very beginning. The point is not to become dependent on any particular ritual – meditation should lead to inner freedom, not increased dependence – but to give your practice a chance to take root. Once you have acquired the knack and the seed of meditation has sprouted, you will be able to meditate at any time, anywhere.

Practical guidelines

We live in an age when there are so many competing demands on our time that the first challenge we might have to overcome in establishing a practice of meditation is simply to find time for it. If this strikes a chord then you may need to rid yourself of the idea that spending time exploring your inner self is in some way selfish. Of course, if by meditating you are going to deprive your partner or children of the only time in the day they might get to see you then it could be considered selfish, but in reality the reverse is likely to be true. By devoting a little time to meditation – and if ten minutes is all you can spare, it will still make a difference – you are likely to have more energy to handle all the demands of your busy lifestyle. Give yourself permission to meditate, at least for a trial period, and make it a priority. Then meditation will happen.

For most people, and especially the time-pressured, the most realistic option is to fix regular times or slots in the day – but without being obsessive about it. Many teachers have advised that dawn and dusk are the most auspicious times of day to meditate – times when the cells of the body are changing and are most receptive to the meditative energy. This is an appealing prospect for anyone living in parts of the world where there is not too much variation in the time of the rising and setting of the sun, but if you live in Alaska or Norway you may find yourself sitting for meditation at very changeable and strange times of day. Better settle for first thing in the morning, when the mind is relatively clear, or last thing at night, which can set you up for a good night's sleep. If you find this difficult, experiment to find a time that suits you and will fit in with your daily routine – the quality of meditation can vary at different times. If possible, you should allow an hour or two to pass after eating before you meditate, longer after a large meal, to allow time for digestion. You are likely to be less alert just after eating and may well end up meditating on your distended waistline rather than your inner self! Try to ensure that you will remain undisturbed while you meditate. Put the answering machine on and let family or friends know you would like to be left in peace – and use earplugs if necessary.

If you have not meditated before it is best to build up slowly the amount of time you devote to meditation rather than set yourself impossible targets that you will not be able to keep. Five minutes of daily focussed attention is much better than an hour spent in a hazy daydream. Start by meditating for a minimum of ten minutes, and a maximum of thirty, once or twice a day. Wind up by sitting quietly for a few minutes to acknowledge your meditation and help integrate the experience into the rest of your life.

Creating the right environment

The Buddha famously attained enlightenment while seated beneath the Bodhi Tree, a descendant of which still flourishes on the very site where he sat in meditation 2,500 years ago. The site is the most important place of pilgrimage for Buddhists and, as anyone who has ever been touched by the charged atmosphere that pervades sacred places where people have prayed and meditated intensely will understand, is considered holy ground.

The power of your meditation may not (yet) match the Buddha's, but creating your own 'sacred space' for meditation, however humble, can really boost your practice. When you sit regularly in the same place for meditation, the place becomes meditative either by association or, as some would have it, by absorbing particles charged with the vibration of the meditative energy that has been released into the environment. For the same reason many teachers recommend reserving a special mat or blanket to sit on for meditation and wearing the same clothes. It may also help you to get in the right frame of mind.

Choose a quiet room or corner where you will be warm and comfortable and make it into your own personal meditation temple with the help of anything that inspires you – incense, candlelight, flowers, pictures of saints or gurus, uplifting music or chanting. Try to reserve it solely for meditation and you will find the more you use it, the more the atmosphere will build up. When you sit there, you will slip into meditation simply and naturally.

If this is not possible, and meditation is not coming easily to you, follow the Buddha's example and find a tree to sit under, or sit by a lake or a waterfall. Nature can never fail to inspire. Gaze up at the sky and watch the clouds pass by. Look at the early morning dew on each blade of grass. Almost anything can become the source for inspiration and meditation – and once you take the first steps, you set in motion an irreversible process. In the end it will be meditation that chases you, rather than you seeking meditation.

An urn of incense burning in the Emperor Jade Pagoda, Ho Chi Minh City, Vietnam. Incense can help to create a meditative atmosphere.

Lotus

Padmasana, or the lotus position, in which the Buddha is classically depicted, is the very symbol of meditation. Each foot is placed on the opposite thigh, which provides a stable base from which the meditator can remain completely still yet alert. Combining strength, grace, poise and balance, the pose roots the sitting bones into the ground while the trunk extends upwards, the crown of the head reaching towards the sky. This symbolizes the linking of heaven and earth, God and man, the particular with the universal. By remaining still in the lotus position meditation arises naturally.

Of all the postures, two are special. The first is the perfect posture, the second is the lotus posture. *Yoga Sutra*, Patanjali

Posture

An important factor in creating the right environment for meditation is your sitting posture. Any comfortable cross-legged position is good for meditation, but if you have sufficient flexibility in your hips and knees – and most people can develop this – the classical meditation positions are excellent because with practice you will be able to sit perfectly still in them for long stretches of time. The mind and body are inextricably linked and physical stillness is conducive to a quiet heart and a still mind. Keeping the back relaxed but upright is considered the most vital aspect of any meditation position, the spinal nerves being at the centre of most physical movements. From the correct posture, correct breathing naturally follows. From these two flow the right frame of mind for meditation to arise spontaneously – quiet, calm and watchful.

If you can sit comfortably in the lotus this is ideal, as the spine elongates upwards quite naturally in this position, hence its value for meditation. It is also a relaxing posture once your hips, knees and ankles gain sufficient flexibility. However, most Westerners, accustomed to sitting in chairs, tend to be a bit stiff in these areas and may not be able to sit in the posture without working on loosening up the joints. Never force your limbs into this position as you can easily damage your knees by doing so, and build up the length of time you sit in it gradually.

If the lotus is too difficult you might like to begin with the half lotus, an easier sitting position. Another alternative is the perfect posture (*siddhasana*), a classic meditation position highly praised in yogic literature. Even if you feel some dis-

comfort to begin with, it is well worth persevering with the classic sitting positions because they provide a firm and stable base for meditation. Start sitting in them for just a minute or two, building up minute by minute, if you can.

If none of these options are possible, sit on the floor in a simple cross-legged position. Alternatively, you can kneel with your buttocks on your heels, or sit on a chair – the straight-backed, dining-table variety. Again, the most important thing in any position is to hold your spine comfortably upright, tucking your chin in and holding your shoulders down. Imagine a golden thread extending all the way from your tail-bone along your spine and up through the crown of your head, gently pulling you up towards the ceiling.

The hands can be placed on the knees, or clasped or folded in the lap. In yogic traditions they are generally placed on the thighs, with the thumbs and forefingers touching – a gesture symbolizing consciousness and said to seal in the inner spiritual energy. In Zen and other Buddhist traditions the hands are usually folded in the lap with the back of one hand resting in the palm of the other, fingers stretched out and palms touching, in a gesture symbolizing concentration. In most traditions, the eyes are closed during meditation, but in some Buddhist traditions they are kept half open, with the gaze lowered so that it rests on the floor about a metre away, yet not focussed on anything – concentration is still directed inwards. This helps keep meditators alert and awake and prevents distracting images arising during meditation.

Half lotus

Easier than the full lotus is the half lotus position, in which one foot is placed beneath the opposite thigh and the other foot is placed on top of the opposite thigh. An even simpler version – sometimes called the quarter lotus – involves placing the top foot over the opposite calf while the other foot lies under the opposite thigh. A better position, with a straighter back and the knees resting more easily on the ground, will be achieved if you place a cushion or folded blanket beneath you.

Siddhasana

Siddhasana, also known as the perfect posture, is said to burst open the door to liberation and bring about the acquisition of miraculous powers. It is also said to be highly beneficial for people practising celibacy, helping them to control their desires and turn their minds inwards. In this position the left heel is placed against the perineum and the right against the pubic bone, and the toes of the right foot are tucked in between the calf and thigh of the left leg. If the knees do not reach the ground, place a firm cushion or block beneath the buttocks. This posture is reputed to help awaken the inner spiritual energy, bringing meditation more easily.

Cross-legged position

This is an easy and comfortable position for most people. Placing a cushion beneath you to raise your hips will improve your posture. As with all meditation positions, it is important to sit in an upright but relaxed position, with your head, neck and trunk in a vertical line, yet maintaining the natural curve of the spine.

Posture should be stable and comfortable.   *Yoga Sutra,* Patanjali

Kneeling position

Kneeling with your buttocks resting on the insides of your feet is a good alternative to sitting cross-legged as it is easier to keep the back straight in this position. For extra comfort, or if your buttocks do not reach your feet, place a cushion on your heels. A variation of this position is to take the feet apart and sit in between them, keeping your knees together, and using a cushion below your buttocks if they do not reach the floor.

Chair position

If you are more comfortable sitting on a chair, choose one with a firm seat and a straight back. To encourage an upright spine, place a cushion at the back of the chair so you are sitting to the front of the seat. For extra support, place another cushion between your back and the back of the chair. Place your feet firmly on the floor, hip-width apart, with your knees directly above them and your hands in your lap.

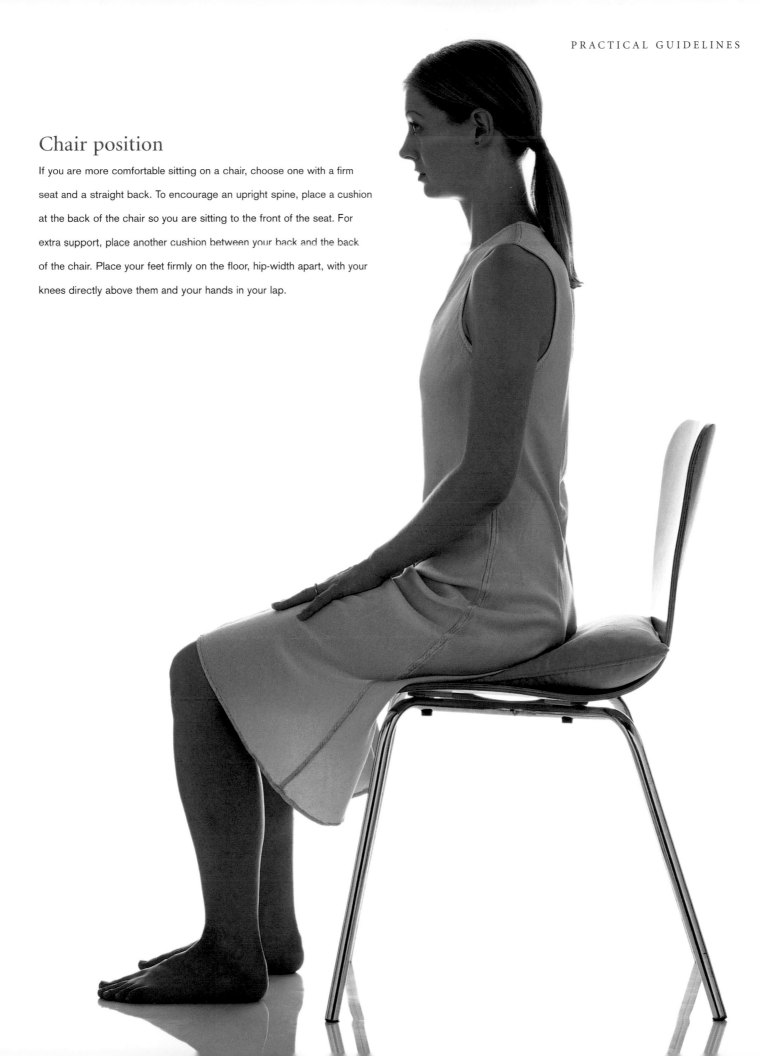

Relaxation

Although meditation produces a relaxing effect in itself, consciously relaxing the body and mind at the outset helps you go deeper into meditation more easily and rapidly. Relax your body with the mind and the breath, scanning it from head to toe and mentally relaxing each part of the body: toes, feet, legs, hips, and so on, up to the shoulders, neck, throat, face and the crown of the head. Then mentally relax the internal organs. Wherever you find tension spots simply breathe into them. Breathe in energy, breathe out tension. Once you have let go of any tension in your body, relax the mind, observing without interference or judgement the thoughts and emotions that float in and out of your consciousness. As you move into meditation maintain this relaxed awareness as you settle into the stillness of the heart.

Breathing

A relaxed and upright sitting posture encourages a quiet, even rhythm of breathing that calms the mind and helps you slip into meditation. Many forms of meditation involve focussing on the breath, and some involve complex breathing techniques, but generally speaking, you should allow the breath to come and go naturally as you meditate, without disturbing its rhythm.

As you go deeper into meditation you may find changes to the breathing process occur spontaneously. The breath may become slower and shallower, to the point where it seems to virtually stop. This can be a little unnerving, but is actually a sign that the mind is becoming very still and you are going into deep meditation. Try to go with it rather than pull back, and see where it takes you. You may find the gaps between the inhalations and exhalations open up. If so, gently shift the focus of your attention to that opening space. Another typical experience of awakened inner energy is breath retention, sometimes in combination with a series of rapid breath expulsions from the abdomen. This process is formalized in the yogic practice of bellows breathing, or *bhastrika pranayama*, which is used to rouse the kundalini, the inner spiritual energy. Because incorrect practice can cause dizziness or nausea the technique is best learnt from a teacher unless it takes place automatically, in which case try to relax and trust in the inner process of purification, and allow these changes to take place without interference.

The spirit of meditation

Much more important than where you meditate or when you meditate, or even what technique you use, is the spirit in which you do it. The practices of invoking grace (this could be the grace of your inner guide or inner self, your God, your guru or a saint), and of dedicating your meditation (say, for world peace or for the enlightenment of all beings) are powerful ways to ensure that your meditation becomes more than just a way to find temporary peace of mind or relaxation.

Cherishing meditation, and carrying it out with tenderness, interest and creativity, opens the heart and allows the sweetness of one's inner self to be experienced. People who get a lot from meditation are not necessarily the ones who have incredible experiences of seeing flashing lights or exotic visions, but those who skilfully integrate their experiences of inner calm and joy, and the feeling of being at one with the world, into their everyday lives. To sustain this awareness there is no substitute for regular meditation followed by a few minutes of sitting quietly, acknowledging your meditation and allowing the meditative state to permeate your day-to-day consciousness. In this way you create space for the subtle process of personal evolution and transformation to take place. This is the real miracle of meditation.

A path and a gateway have no meaning
or use once the objective is in sight.

Ali al-Hujwiri, 11th century Sufi master

Just as the many arches of this palace all lead towards the light, the various

meditation techniques are portals leading into the inner realm.

Some people seem able to settle naturally into the stillness of pure awareness. For them techniques can be by-passed – they would only be a hindrance. But left to our own devices, the vast majority of us would find ourselves groping in the dark and making no progress at all. We need a handle to hang on to as we delve into the innermost recesses of our consciousness, and this is where techniques can help us. They give the mind something to do, something to focus on. This helps us move beyond the constant stream of inner thoughts and mental chatter to the space of stillness within. Different techniques are like different gateways

Choosing a technique

into this inner realm, and to begin with meditation is practised by focussing attention on whatever technique is chosen. When meditation happens, techniques fall away.

Most of the methods described have been used for thousands of years, handed down from teacher to student in a long line. Yet they remain fresh and effective if you can make them your own. Like new shoes, you may need to wear them for a few weeks before they mould themselves to the shape of your feet and become a perfect fit. Some techniques, like some shoes, may never feel really comfortable. Have a browse and if you see something that attracts you, try it on for size.

Meditation is the complete identification with whatever techniques you are employing.

Chogyam Trungpa, 20th century Tibetan Buddhist teacher

All too often the quest for the 'right' technique turns into the meditator's Holy Grail. Forgetting that techniques are means, not ends, we get fixated on what is the right technique to use or the best mantra to recite, worrying that if we make the wrong choice it will somehow blight our entire spiritual life. In fact, what is really paralysing is the indecision, so try to avoid spending a disproportionate amount of time deciding which is *the one*. Unless you have been initiated into a particular technique by an empowered teacher (in which case it is likely to bear fruit for you more quickly), there is nothing particularly sacred about techniques. They are simply tools for drawing you inward to the discovery of your true self. Techniques provide support for the mind as it settles into the open space of its own essential nature, and can be discarded once meditation arises and you float free in the expanse of consciousness. Real meditation is total presence, not reciting a mantra or visualizing a lighted candle.

The simple answer to the question of which technique to use is: whatever works for you. Anything that puts you on the road and takes you some of the distance is fine. Other than that, it comes down to preference and opportunity. Although some techniques may be more effective for the majority of people, in the long run whether you make your own way by bicycle or on foot, get chauffeur driven in a limo or ride pillion, or hop on a train and catnap most of the way, hardly matters so long as you are headed in the right direction. Simple techniques are as effective as complicated ones if they

point you towards your destination. Ultimately, no techniques are needed at all.

Before simply sitting and going into free fall, however, you need to learn the basics. Just as a musician must learn the tools of his or her trade – notation, fingering and so on – before he or she can successfully improvise, so newcomers to meditation are best advised to follow tried-and-tested approaches to meditation. This may require a bit of experimentation, but usually when you find a technique that is good for you it will somehow just click and feel right. Then you have to make the technique your own, turn it into an individual and personal experience. People know when they have found a way that works for them – it feels natural and enjoyable. This does not necessarily mean sticking with it for ever, any more than you would stay in a relationship that has come to a natural close, or using it so exclusively that you stop experimenting with other methods. Play around, have fun, and see where it takes you. Sooner or later you will have to drop the technique and move beyond it.

This 5th century Christian mosaic showing the baptism of Christ, surrounded by the Apostles, acts in a similar way to a mandala, drawing the eye inwards, and could be used in a visual meditation. It can be seen on the vault of the dome of the Battistero Neoniano Church, in Ravenna, Italy, and would have been gazed at by early Christians during worship.

God is the breath of all breaths.

Kabir

The breath is the life force, the most fundamental expression of our being, and a wide variety of meditation techniques are built around it. Most of these methods are simple and natural, and because they are neutral in respect of religion or philosophy – although practised within almost all traditions – they have universal appeal.

The breath is intimately connected with physical, mental and emotional states. People breathe quietly and evenly when they are relaxed, whereas if they are anxious or angry their breathing quickens and becomes shallow, irregular and often

Breath awareness

noisy. At moments of suspense or intense physical effort we hold our breath, maximizing the energy available to us. We instinctively understand this link between the breath and the mind, and use it to cope with strong emotions or to handle difficult situations. Deep breathing is well-known as one of the most effective stressbusters in the universe. By taking a few long deep breaths, focussing attention on the inhalation and the exhalation, the breath settles down naturally and becomes regular, and we begin to feel calmer and more centred.

In meditation no attempt is made to regulate the flow or rhythm of breath. It becomes smoother and more even of its own accord, without any form of conscious control. Breathe naturally, as you would normally. If you find the pattern of your breathing changing spontaneously in meditation, perhaps becoming slower, finer or shallower, or being retained involuntarily, let it be without interference. This is perfectly natural and a sign that meditation is progressing.

The meditation exercise opposite combines several breath-awareness techniques, starting off by using the breath to help you relax physically. Other ways of centring on the breath in meditation include observing the rise and fall of the abdomen as you breathe in and breathe out, and focussing on the sensation at the tip of your nostrils as the breath flows in and out of the body. Counting the breath is a popular meditation practice used in Zen and other forms of Buddhism. The breaths are counted from one to ten, either on the exhalation or the inhalation, and then the procedure is repeated throughout the meditation.

Focussing on the breath is an ancient practice and makes a very good starting point for meditation. Awareness of the breath can also be combined with other meditation techniques such as the recitation of a mantra, or practising the *hamsa* technique described on pages 152–5.

How dull it is to pause, to make
   an end,
To rust unburnish'd, not to shine
   in use!
As tho' to breathe were life.
   Life piled on life
Were all too little, and of one
   to me
Little remains: but every hour
   is saved
From that eternal silence,
   something more,
A bringer of new things.

Ulysses, Alfred, Lord Tennyson

Watching the breath

Read the meditation instructions through completely once or twice before you begin. You may find it helpful to record them, but be sure to leave plenty of space between each instruction.

Sit comfortably in any cross-legged position, or on a chair if you prefer with your feet flat on the floor. Hold your back, head and neck erect yet relaxed. Tuck in your chin and place your hands in your lap or on your thighs. With the weight of your body centred over your sitting bones, feel these bones pressing down and your spine elongating, as though an invisible string were lifting you from the base of your spine through the crown of your head towards the ceiling. A cushion placed beneath you to raise your hips will help keep the back in an upright position, increasing the flow of meditative energy circulating through the body. Close or half-close your eyes and spend a few moments consciously relaxing your body. Scan it for any pockets of tension and relax with the help of your breath, breathing in energy, breathing out tension.

Now bring your awareness lightly to the movement of the breath, without disturbing its natural rhythm. Allow it to flow freely and let your mind flow with it. Follow the breath as it enters and leaves your body, watching any images and feelings that arise and subside without comment, letting them drift past like clouds in the sky. If you find your attention has wandered, gently bring it back to the breath without trying to shut out thoughts or fantasies. Just keep returning to the breath, dissolving into the breath.

To concentrate the mind you may find it helpful to count breaths. Beginning with the first exhalation, count from one to ten on each outgoing breath, then start over again. If you lose count, gently bring your attention back to the breath and start counting from one again.

At the end of the session open your eyes slowly and sit quietly for a few moments, acknowledging your meditation and allowing it to permeate your everyday consciousness.

You should always repeat the mantra with the
understanding that the mantra, the goal of the mantra,
and the repeater of the mantra are one.

Swami Muktananda

Stones engraved with the Tibetan mantra *om mane padme hum* in Ladakh, India.

The practice of reciting or concentrating on a syllable, word or phrase is perhaps the most widespread of all meditation techniques and is said to be the easiest way to self-realization. The technique can be traced back to the Vedas, India's most ancient sacred literature, but in the 1960s it was popularized by the teachings of the Maharishi Mahesh Yogi, who brought his method of Transcendental Meditation® to the West. The Maharishi's approach to mantra meditation does not involve accepting any beliefs and it is widely practised by people of all cultures and religions with great success. Meditators following his method are given a specially

Mantra meditation

selected Sanskrit word that has no meaning for them, together with instructions as to how to repeat it. Essentially the same method is used within various spiritual traditions, especially yoga, Tibetan Buddhism and Sufism, and increasingly amongst Christians and people who do not subscribe to any particular philosophy or school of thought. Whether sacred or secular, the sounds and words used in meditation are usually referred to as mantras, a word borrowed from Sanskrit, the ancient language of India. Strictly speaking, however, a mantra is used in the context of Hinduism or Buddhism, denoting a sacred utterance that embodies spiritual power and can draw the repeater back to its source.

According to legend the traditional mantras used by yogis were originally revealed to sages deep in meditation as inner vibrations. The syllables and words recited as mantras are approximations of these subtle sounds and can be thought of as the outer casing of the pure vibratory forms. They have been handed down from teacher to disciple over thousands of years and are charged with numinous power, each syllable vibrating with divine energy. By chanting a sacred mantra out loud or silently contemplating it, the meditator becomes imbued with the power embedded within it. His or her mind will then be drawn inwards quite naturally and become centred on the self. For the full potency of a mantra to be realized it should be empowered and imparted by an enlightened teacher.

The syllable *aum* is the bow and one's self is the arrow.
The target is the Ultimate Reality.   *Mundaka Upanishad*

The sacred syllable *om* has been painted on the rock from which this temple, near the peak of Golconda in Hyderabad, India, has been cut.

Om (aum) and other sacred mantras

Of all sacred mantras, the best known is *om*, the supreme Hindu mantra that dates back to Vedic times. Like all sacred mantras, it is regarded as a divine revelation and is said to be the soundless sound from which the entire universe arises, and through which it vibrates eternally. Its practical application is wide-ranging, so as well as being used as a mantra it is often placed at the beginning and end of prayers, with the sense of 'verily' or 'so be it', in much the same way as Christians use the word 'Amen'. *Om* is often combined with other mantras to reinforce their power. One of the best known of these is the traditional Indian mantra *om namah shivaya*, which is said to be the great redeeming mantra. It literally means 'Om, salutations to Shiva', but can be broadly interpreted as honouring the divine spark in the heart of each of us, Shiva being understood as the inner self of all. Another famous mantra is the Tibetan Buddhist formula *om mani padme hum*. This translates literally as 'Om, the jewel in the lotus', but is so full of meaning and significance that one author, Lama Anagarika Govinda, devoted over three hundred pages to analysing it. Amongst its many nuances of meaning, *mani*, meaning jewel, symbolizes our innermost essence, the pure being sometimes known in Buddhism as the Void. This is uncovered when the mind is still and the intervening layers of consciousness penetrated. *Padme*, meaning lotus, symbolizes the spiritual unfolding that must take place to reach *mani*. *Hum*, like *om*, is untranslatable, but symbolizes our potential for enlightenment, and the truth of the void enclosed within the unfurling petals of the non-void. The mantra is said to draw the repeater inwards and enable him or her to tap into higher levels of consciousness.

When *om* is used on its own rather than in combination it is often repeated as three separate syllables *a-u-m* (*aah-ooh-mmm*). Great spiritual power is attributed both to the whole word and to these three individual sounds. *Om* can also be used as a yantra – the visual equivalent of a mantra – and used as an object of visual meditation.

Although the 'science' of mantra is most developed in Hindu and Buddhist traditions, many others use the technique of repeating a mantra. The various names of God can make potent mantras, as can short prayers or phrases from sacred texts. According to the Old Testament the personal name of God represented by the Hebrew letters Y H V H (*Yahweh*) is too sacred to be vocalized, but within Judaism other names, such as Elohim or Jehovah, can be used. The Hebrew letters themselves have mystical connotations and are meditated on singly or in combination. Choices for practising Christians might include *maranatha*, the Aramaic for 'Come Lord', or any of the suggestions from the section on Christian Mysticism (pages 109–113). In Islamic meditation, the devotional practice of *dhikr*, the recitation of names and attributes of God, or of sacred Koranic passages, has an important place. The first line of the Koran, *la ilaha illa'llah* ('There is no God but Allah'), is often used as a mantra by Sufis, as is the repetition of Allah, Allah.

Neutral and non-religious mantras

Followers of spiritual traditions are usually drawn to sacred mantras invested with divine power, promising inner evolution and transformation, but to the non-believer these are nothing more than sounds and syllables that aid concentration and help block out other thoughts. This view is backed up by evidence showing that repetition of any sound or word, regardless of meaning, can induce a state of relaxation. It is well to remember, however, that the purpose of mantra repetition is not to achieve the kind of hypnotic state that can occur as a result of mindless repetition. Self-hypnosis is not meditation. Meditation, unlike hypnosis, is a state of full awareness in which the mind is still, but fully present. Yet without using sacred mantras profound states of consciousness may be achieved, as Alfred, Lord Tennyson, the celebrated English poet, discovered. In a letter to a Mr B.P. Blood he writes of:

'*...a kind of waking trance – this for lack of a better word – I have frequently had, quite up from boyhood, when I have been all alone. This has come upon me through repeating my own name to myself silently, till all at once, as it were out of the intensity of the consciousness of individuality, individuality itself seemed to dissolve and fade away into boundless being, and this is not a confused state but the clearest, the surest of the surest, utterly beyond words – where death was an almost laughable impossibility – the loss of personality (if so it were) seeming no extinction, but the only true life. I am ashamed of my feeble description. Have I not said the state is utterly beyond words?*'

You could do a lot worse than follow in the footsteps of Tennyson and try repeating your own name, as he did with such spectacular results, if you want to experiment with mantra meditation but do not feel comfortable with the beliefs associated with sacred mantras. Otherwise choose any word, phrase or sound that you feel at home with.

More than once when I
Sat all alone, revolving in myself
The word that is the symbol of myself,
The mortal limit of the Self was loosed,
And passed into the nameless, as a cloud
Melts into heaven.

The Ancient Sage, Alfred, Lord Tennyson

A procession of Hare Krishnas chanting their mantra in the streets of Barcelona, Spain.

Using a mantra

Mantras can be used in many different ways and are often chanted out loud by religious devotees such as those of the Krishna Consciousness Movement, who have become a familiar sight in the streets of American and European cities with their chant of 'Hare Krishna, Hare Krishna, Krishna Krishna, Hare Hare, Hare Rama, Hare Rama, Rama Rama, Hare Hare' repeated over and over again. Chanting out loud is said to purify the inner and outer atmosphere, to open the heart and it makes a good way to prepare for meditation. During meditation itself, however, it is better to repeat a simply think it, ideally in combination with the rhythm of the breath, repeating it once on the inhalation and once on the exhalation. Listen to the sound of the syllables as you repeat your mantra, so that your whole awareness becomes saturated with it. If you are visually oriented you may also find it helpful to try visualizing each syllable of the mantra in written form – perhaps in letters of golden light – as you silently pronounce them.

Repeating a mantra

Read the meditation instructions through completely once or twice before you begin. You may find it helpful to record them, or the parts of them relevant to the mantra you are repeating, but be sure to leave plenty of space between each instruction.

Sit comfortably in any cross-legged position, or on a chair if you prefer with your feet flat on the floor. Hold your back, head and neck erect yet relaxed. Tuck in your chin and place your hands in your lap or on your thighs. With the weight of your body centred over your sitting bones, feel these bones pressing down and your spine elongating, as though an invisible string were lifting you from the base of your spine through the crown of your head towards the ceiling. A cushion placed beneath you will raise your hips and help keep the back in an upright position, increasing the flow of meditative energy circulating through the body. Close or half-close your eyes and spend a few moments consciously relaxing your body. Scan it for any pockets of tension and relax with the help of your breath, breathing in energy, breathing out tension.

Now begin to repeat the mantra *om namah shivaya*, or any sound or mantra of your choosing, silently to yourself at your normal speaking tempo or slightly slower. If you wish, you can co-ordinate the mantra with your breathing. If you are repeating a four- to six-syllabled mantra such as *om namah shivaya*, repeat it once as you breathe in, and once as you breathe out. If you are using a one- or two-syllabled word or phrase such as 'peace', or 'Allah', you can repeat it two or even three times on each breath. Longer mantras or prayers may need to be split between the inhalation and exhalation – for example, breathing in to the words 'Jesus Christ, Son of God', and breathing out to 'Have mercy upon us'.

Breathe naturally as you repeat the mantra without disturbing the normal rhythm, but if changes to the pattern of your breathing occur spontaneously let them be. Allow the mantra to flow with the breath and as you continue to repeat it, bring your awareness to the sound of the syllables and immerse yourself in them. If you find your attention wandering, gently bring it back to the mantra, without trying to shut out thoughts or fantasies. Just keep returning to the mantra, feeling yourself surrounded by the field of force created by the energy of the mantra's sound vibrations.

At the end of the session open your eyes slowly and sit quietly for a few moments, acknowledging your meditation and allowing it to permeate your everyday consciousness.

He is lauded as a swan (*hamsa*) who knows the swan
that is stationed in the heart and endowed with the
unstruck sound, the self-luminous consciousness-bliss.

Brahma-Vidya-Upanishad

Ancient yogic texts describe the sound of the breath itself as a mantra, entering the body with the sound *ha* and leaving it with the sound *sa*. At the transition point between the incoming breath and the outgoing breath, where the *ha* merges inside and before the *sa* arises, the nasal *m* occurs, so that with each full inhalation and exhalation the sound *hamsa* ('swan') can be heard. Because the hamsa mantra is spontaneously and effortlessly repeated by every living being, whether they are aware of it or not, it is known as the natural mantra. Because it

happens by itself, without being

The hamsa technique

mechanically recited either mentally

or out loud, it is also known as the unrecited recitation. The art of practising the hamsa technique is simply to become aware of the breath and to listen to the subtle sound it makes as it comes in and goes out of the body. The hamsa mantra is also known as the *so'ham* mantra because the sequence *hamsa-hamsa-hamsa* can be heard in reverse as *so'ham-so'ham-so'ham*, meaning 'I am that', and symbolizing the identity of the individual self with the infinite. In this way, with each breath the body reaffirms its own true nature.

The hamsa technique is said to be enormously powerful, helping to arouse the kundalini, the dormant spiritual energy within the individual. Through this process the breathing becomes more subtle and the mind will become very still. With practice you will find that the space between the breaths will open up, but let it happen naturally, without forcing it. This is the space of the self. Enter into it.

Practising the hamsa technique

Read the meditation instructions through completely once or twice before you begin. You may find it helpful to record them but be sure to leave plenty of space between each instruction.

Sit comfortably in any cross-legged position, or on a chair with your feet flat on the floor. Hold your back, head and neck erect yet relaxed. Tuck in your chin and place your hands in your lap or on your thighs. With the weight of your body centred over your sitting bones, feel these bones pressing down and your spine elongating, as though an invisible string were lifting you from the base of your spine through the crown of your head towards the ceiling. A cushion placed beneath you will raise your hips and help keep the back in an upright position, increasing the flow of meditative energy circulating through the body. Close or half-close your eyes and spend a few moments consciously relaxing your body. Scan it for any pockets of tension and relax with the help of your breath, breathing in energy, breathing out tension.

Now bring your awareness to the movement of the breath without disturbing its natural rhythm. Notice where the inhalation and exhalation arise and dissolve. Follow the movement of the breath and listen to the sounds it makes. As you breathe in, you should hear a sound like *ham* or *hum*, and as you breathe out, hear the sound *sa* or *so*. Between these two movements, in the region of the heart, is a point of complete stillness before the pendulum of the breath swings back. Softly focus your attention on this turning point, where the incoming breath subsides and the outgoing breath arises. Neither lengthen this stillness nor curtail it, simply watch it. When the exhalation takes place, flow with it to the still point in the outer space at a distance of about twelve fingers from the tip of the nose, where it subsides and the next inhalation arises. Now focus on the outer space where the breath is briefly suspended without deliberately elongating it. As you rest in the pause between the breaths it will naturally open up and you will experience an expansion of consciousness.

If you find your attention wandering gently bring it back to the breath, without trying to shut out thoughts or fantasies. Bring your awareness back to the continuous repetition of the sounds *ham* and *sa*, and the contemplation of the space between them.

At the end of the session open your eyes slowly and sit quietly for a few moments, acknowledging your meditation and allowing it to permeate your everyday consciousness.

To see a World in a Grain of Sand,
And a Heaven in a Wild Flower,
Hold Infinity in the palm of your hand,
And Eternity in an hour.

Auguries of Innocence, William Blake

William Blake was gifted with the spiritual vision of the mystic and the genius to transmit his experience through poetry and art. The famous opening lines of his *Auguries of Innocence* encapsulate in the most poetic language the way even ordinary objects and forms, if we really look at them, can open up the doors of perception and give us a glimpse of the infinite, the eternal reality.

Visualization utilizes the natural ability of the mind to create and recreate images, and in so doing, to transcend them and tap into higher states of consciousness. Many children possess a remarkable

Visualization techniques

ability to generate mental images and some have visions, as did the young Blake. Unlike most of us, however, Blake retained the ability up until the end of his life, the richness of his inner life being the source of his genius as an artist. The facility of creating images tends to wane as we grow older and the incredible array of visual imagery that surrounds us today in the form of television, the cinema, computer games and technology has to a certain extent impoverished us and further impaired our ability to visualize creatively. With practice our innate ability for visualization can be restored.

Religious and symbolic imagery is used in most traditions to transform consciousness and encourage spiritual development, as we have seen. In the Christian church religious art depicting the life of Christ, the Virgin Mary and the saints is used as an aid to contemplation, both in the devotional paintings of the West and in the icons of the Eastern Orthodox Church (pages 109–113). Mystical symbols occur in many traditions, such as the Kabbalistic tree of life (page 107), the Taoist yin-yang symbol (pages 98–99) and the chakras of yoga (pages 64–65). Mystical diagrams have reached their greatest complexity and artistic splendour in the mandalas of Tantric Buddhism, with their brilliant colours and rich symbolism. Mandalas, which are discussed in more detail below, are circular designs representing the cosmos and the individual psyche, the most famous being the Buddhist Wheel of Life (page 83).

Visualization is the most characteristic method of meditation used in Tantra, both Buddhist and yogic, and is also used in various other forms of yoga. Images of such complexity as the mandala are not, however, necessary and beginners are advised to practise visualization using a single object. As visualization abilities develop, more complicated images can be used. Gazing at the flame of a candle in a darkened room is a time-honoured way to start. Just as a lit fire in a hearth provides a natural focus, so the eyes are naturally drawn to the brightness of the flame, and the image is easy to retain. After a while the eyes are closed and the flame is internalized, this being the more subtle practice. As visualization skills develop, it becomes easier to hold the image of the flame or other object steadily in the mind's eye. Eventually, external images can be dispensed with entirely. Incidentally, although there are certain similarities, meditative techniques of visualization should not be confused with the techniques of creative visualization, which use positive affirmations, mental images and guided fantasies as an aid to self-development, healing, achieving specific goals and so on.

As progress is made in visualization, perception is heightened – people sometimes report really 'seeing' things for the first time. A dewdrop on a blade of grass will be seen to have an almost magical beauty that gives as much aesthetic pleasure as the most exquisite rose or diamond. The ultimate goal, of course, is to see the whole phenomenal world as it really is, all of the time. This is enlightenment.

Smooth stones, such as these, make an attractive focus for visual meditation, especially for people who prefer to avoid religious symbols.

Choosing an object or image

Focal points for visual meditation can range from simple objects such as a blade of grass to images of great complexity. A candle flame against a darkened background is a classic focal point, although you should be careful not to strain your eyes, but any image or object can be used and visualized using the same method as described in the candle-gazing exercise on the following page. Popular choices include:

● **Natural objects and features** such as stones, leaves or flowers, mountains, waterfalls or the sky. Small objects have the advantage of fitting nicely into any meditation environment, and are best placed on a table or stand roughly level with your eyes. Other advantages of natural objects are that they are usually attractive to the eye and tend to be free of religious or mystical association. Exceptions to the rule include the lotus flower, which is portrayed in the mandalas and chakras of Buddhism and yoga, and enjoys a rich symbolism. It represents the mystical centre or heart, and stands for spiritual enlightenment, the perfect beauty of its form emerging from the muddy waters in which it has taken root. In the West the rose has a parallel symbology, again representing the mystical centre or heart and standing for perfection and completion.

● **Geometrical shapes and colours** can also be used to great effect and both play a major role in the creation of mandalas and other mystical diagrams, and in the kasina meditations discussed below. The circle appears in all traditions, from the most primitive to the most sophisticated, symbolizing the self or psyche, and pointing to the ultimate wholeness of life.

● **Universal symbols** such as the egg, which finds a place in most symbolic traditions. The cosmic egg represents potentiality, the seed of life, primordial matter. The essence of these beliefs is embodied in the symbology of the Easter egg, which is an emblem of immortality. A more exotic choice is the phoenix, the fabulous bird that periodically sets fire to itself and rises again from the ashes, representing spiritual as well as physical rebirth.

● **Mystical and religious art and symbols** such as all those mentioned previously and illustrated in the individual descriptions of traditions in Chapter 2 and in 'Mandalas and Yantras' on pages 166-167. Meditation on these images may include subtler forms of visualization, such as focussing on the central point of a mandala, which represents 'the still point of the turning world', the potential energy that is the origin of the unfolded reality of the phenomenal world.

● **Mystical syllables** Certain sounds, letters and words, such as the mantra *om*, are said to correspond with specific psychic realities. As well as being repeated out loud or mentally as mantras, the letters of these sounds can simultaneously or separately be visualized with the inner eye in the written form.

● **Inner imagery** The most refined form of visualization, which involves no external image or object, is that of inner lights and other internally created or manifested imagery. Simple visualizations of this kind are described in the section on *dharanas* below, and illustrated in the meditation exercise on page 161, which is a more subtle version of the candle-gazing exercise.

Gazing at a candle flame

Read the meditation instructions through completely once or twice before you begin. You may find it helpful to record them but be sure to leave plenty of space between each instruction.

Sit comfortably in a darkened room in any cross-legged position, or on a chair if you prefer, having placed a small lighted candle about a metre away from you and approximately level with your eyes. The room should be free from draughts, so the flame will burn steadily without flickering too much. Hold your back, head and neck erect yet relaxed. Tuck in your chin and place your hands in your lap or on your thighs. With the weight of your body centred over your sitting bones, feel these bones pressing down and your spine elongating. A cushion placed beneath you to raise your hips will help keep the back in an upright position, increasing the flow of meditative energy circulating through the body. Close or half-close your eyes and spend a few moments consciously relaxing your body. Scan it for any pockets of tension and relax with the help of your breath, breathing in energy, breathing out tension.

Now open your eyes and, breathing naturally, focus your attention on the flame. Gaze at it in a steady, relaxed way for a few minutes. Be receptive to the flame, allowing it to reveal itself to you, rather than actively thinking about it. Keep on looking at the flame, even if your eyes begin to water. The practice of gazing at a small object until the eyes water is known in yoga as *trataka*, and is said to cleanse the eyes and tear ducts, improve eyesight and heal eye disorders. As you continue to observe the flame you will discover new qualities in it, new colours. If you find your attention wandering, gently direct it back to the flame without trying to shut out thoughts or fantasies. Keep your eye and facial muscles relaxed throughout.

After two or three minutes, or if you feel any strain in the eyes, lower your eyelids. You will probably find that a strong after-image forms in the space between your eyebrows. Focus on this until it fades, then mentally recreate a clear image of the flame, allowing its aura to illuminate you from within. After a few minutes with your eyelids lowered, gently open your eyes again and repeat the process. Keep alternating between gazing at the candle and visualizing it. To begin with, the image may be difficult to form and may slip away quickly, but with practice you will be able to hold it for longer periods.

At the end of the session open your eyes slowly and sit quietly for a few moments, acknowledging your meditation, feeling yourself filled with light.

I shall light a candle of understanding in thine heart, which shall not be put out. *Apocrypha*

Seeing the light

Light is the most natural and universal symbol of mystical consciousness – we talk of enlightenment or illumination in relation to the experience of spiritual truth. Light has been worshipped since time immemorial, whether in the form of the sun, or in the form of the Supreme, the source of all light, compared in the Bhagavad Gita to 'the light of a thousand suns'.

One of the most simple yet, for many people, most effective forms of meditation is to visualize yourself as being filled with light or enveloped by light. This is a little more subtle than the candle-gazing meditation, but is not complicated and is very relaxing. In the meditation exercise on the right, light is envisaged in the region of the heart centre, but there are many variations on this theme. To see yourself as being filled with light, simply sit for meditation as described opposite, with your eyes closed, and visualize a shaft of pure bright light pouring into the crown of your head and filling your entire body. To visualize yourself enveloped by light, sit as described, with your eyes closed, and imagine that you are surrounded by light – it can be whatever colour you like – white, blue, pink – forming a luminous cocoon all around you.

Visualizing the light in your heart

Sit comfortably as described opposite and close your eyes. Bring your awareness to the movement of the breath, without disturbing its natural rhythm. As you follow the movement of the breath, gently take your attention down to the region of the heart. Feel your breath flowing in and out of the heart.

Now become aware of a subtle glow of light in the centre of your heart. As you go deeper within, breathing in energy, the light grows larger and brighter, like a golden sun illuminating you from within. Feel the rays of its light and warmth filling your entire being and experience yourself as light – pure, golden, spiritual light.

Kasina meditations

The *Visuddhimagga*, or 'Path of Purity', is a fifth century Buddhist work that describes in detail the techniques of meditation used in the Theravada school (see page 85). The ten *kasinas*, 'total fields', which are recommended as subjects for visual meditation are the four elements of earth, water, fire and wind (air); the four colours: blue, yellow, red and white; space and consciousness. Consciousness is traditionally represented by light, which symbolizes the highest state of consciousness – enlightenment. The kasina meditations find a counterpart in the five dharanas (concentration practices) described in the *Hatha-Yoga-Pradipika*, one of the classic texts of hatha yoga, which involves focussing on each of the following: earth, water, fire, air and space.

To meditate on any one of the kasinas the meditator should choose an appropriate physical object as follows:

1   **Earth element** This may be represented by an earthen disc or a dish filled with earth, which should ideally be soft and loose, and free of extraneous matter such as grass, roots, pebbles and so on. If meditating out of doors a ploughed field, soil in a flowerpot or a flowerbed will serve.

2   **Water element** Indoors this can be represented by a glass or bowl filled with water; outdoors by dewdrops, a pond or lake (either perfectly still or with ripples forming), a waterfall, stream, river or the sea.

3   **Fire element** Indoors this can be represented by a candle flame, a fire burning in a hearth or burning embers; outdoors by a bonfire. (Staring directly at the sun is not recommended as it can damage your eyes.)

4   **Wind element** Although it cannot be seen directly, the effects of the wind are evident in the movement of solids, liquids and gases. Indoors meditate in a room where there is some movement of air and watch the leaves of a houseplant caught in a draught, the smoke of an incense stick curling upwards or a light curtain blowing in the breeze at an opened window. Outside you can watch plants swaying in the wind, flags fluttering, clouds drifting past, and so on.

5–8 **The colours: blue, yellow, red and white** These may be represented by any object of the colour being meditated on, or simply by a sheet of paper or disc painted in the chosen colour. For example, for blue choose a blue flower or bowl of flowers arranged so as to appear as a dense mass of blue; a blue cloth; blue paint; a blue plate, and so on. If meditating outside, gaze at the sky, the sea, and so on.

9   **Space** This is represented by the space between objects or by emptiness. If meditating indoors, focus on an empty bowl or other vessel, a stone or sculpture with

a hole in it, a keyhole or an open doorway. If outdoors, focus on the gaps between trees or buildings.

Rocks, like those in this Zen garden in Japan, can also represent the earth element in a kasina meditation.

10 **Consciousness** As mentioned opposite, this is represented by light – the source of illumination or supreme consciousness. Indoors meditate on the light cast by a lamp or spotlight, sunlight coming through a window or the coloured rays of light refracted by a cut glass ball. If outdoors, meditate on the rays of light filtered through foliage, the reflection of light in water or the light of the moon or stars.

The kasina objects are not ends in themselves, but means to achieving the thought-free state associated with higher states of consciousness. Concentrating on a material object acts as a support for the mind, focussing the attention and leading to this inner stillness. The method of meditating on the blue kasina described in the following exercise can easily be adapted for any chosen object and for any of the kasinas.

Visualizing the colour blue

Read the meditation instructions through completely once or twice before you begin. You may find it helpful to record them, but be sure to leave plenty of space between each instruction.

Sit comfortably in any cross-legged position, or on a chair if you prefer with your feet flat on the floor, having placed the blue object of your choice, such as flowers, a disc or a sculpture like the beautiful piece opposite, *At the Hub of Things* by Anish Kapoor, about a metre away from you and approximately level with your eyes. Hold your back, head and neck erect yet relaxed. Tuck in your chin and place your hands in your lap or on your thighs. With the weight of your body centred over your sitting bones, feel these bones pressing down and your spine elongating, as though an invisible string were lifting you from the base of your spine through the crown of your head towards the ceiling. A cushion placed beneath you will raise your hips and help keep your back in an upright position, increasing the flow of meditative energy. Close or half-close your eyes and spend a few moments consciously relaxing your body. Scan it for any pockets of tension and relax with the help of your breath, breathing in energy, breathing out tension.

Now open your eyes and, breathing naturally, focus your attention on the blue object. Gaze at it in a steady, relaxed way for a few minutes, allowing it to imprint itself on your mind, rather than actively thinking about it and its qualities. Keep on looking until your whole consciousness becomes filled with it and your mind is completely immersed in it. If you find your attention wandering, gently direct it back to the colour, without trying to shut out thoughts or fantasies. Keep your eye and facial muscles relaxed throughout.

After a while close your eyes and recreate the blueness internally. Visualize it for as long as you can, then repeat the whole process. Keep alternating between gazing at the object and visualizing the colour for the duration of your meditation. To begin with, it may be difficult to mentally recreate the colour, but with a little practice it will become clearer and stronger, and you will be able to hold it for longer periods. The inner image will eventually be as distinct as the outer reality. As when the eyes are open, allow any thoughts and other images that arise to drift through your mind as you gently bring your attention back to the blueness.

At the end of the session open your eyes slowly and sit quietly for a few moments, acknowledging your meditation and allowing it to permeate your everyday consciousness.

Mandalas and yantras

A *mandala* (Sanskrit for 'circle') is the name given to various circular designs that express universal truth in symbolic form and are used as a focus for meditation. A mandala represents the forces of the cosmos and the individual self, the macrocosm and the microcosm. It maps the process by which the One, represented by the mysterious central point, or *bindu*, becomes the many, and symbolizes the mystical journey back through the layers of consciousness to the experience of pure consciousness or divine unity.

Although the content of a mandala varies from one culture to another, its form is universal and it appears widely as a religious or mystical symbol. Some of the most splendid examples in the Christian church include the Gothic rose windows of cathedrals such as York Minster, the Sachsler Meditation Picture, and ornate paintings and mosaics on the ceilings and floors of churches, such as that illustrated on page 141. The Chinese mirrors that are sometimes known as TLV mirrors, owing to the ornamentation that suggests those letters, are also mandala designs representing the universe, with the central point symbolizing the return to unity consciousness. The form of the mandala design is frequently found in Islamic art, as well as in mythical and alchemical symbolism. When images in the form of a mandala began arising spontaneously in his dreams, the psychologist Carl Jung became interested in them and discovered that some of his patients had similar experiences. From this he concluded that the mandala represents the psyche and forms part of the collective unconscious.

Without any doubt, however, the art of constructing and visualizing mandalas is most developed in Tantric yoga, both Buddhist and Hindu. The mandalas of Tantric Buddhism, such as the famous Buddhist Wheel of Life illustrated on page 83, are elaborate and brilliantly coloured works of art with a complex and rich symbolism, as can be seen from the *thangkas* or religious paintings on which they are often depicted. The act of creating – or even commissioning – a mandala is itself considered a meditative act of great merit, and as well as being drawn or painted, a mandala may be depicted with coloured sand (such as on page 169), constructed three-dimensionally as, for example, the stupas of Tibet or the famous temple of Borabadur in Java, or its image may be constructed mentally. The latter presupposes advanced powers of visualization and would not normally be undertaken except under the guidance of a teacher who would select an appropriate mandala according to the personality and qualities of the student.

A *yantra* – a Sanskrit word literally meaning 'instrument' or 'support' – is a mystical diagram intended as a support for meditation, an instrument for attaining divine consciousness.

The *Om* yantra. A yantra, meaning 'instrument', is a mystical and symbolic diagram that maps the levels and energies of the universe – in this case the energy pattern of the mantra *om*. The visual equivalent of a mantra, a yantra is an instrument for attaining divine consciousness through meditation and is particularly associated with Tantric practices (see page 70).

By comparison with the mandalas of Tibetan Tantra, the yantras of Hindu Tantrism (the most famous of which is the Shri yantra illustrated on page 72–73, followed by the *om* yantra on the previous page) are relatively simple. Most yantras are mandalas, or circular forms, and like the Tibetan mandalas can be constructed in a three-dimensional form. The main difference between Buddhist mandalas and yantras is that the latter tend to be more pictorial. A yantra is a geometrical design, typically composed of a square surround, within which are concentric circles, some of which are framed with lotus petals, concentric or intersecting triangles, and a central point known as the *bindu*. The bindu is the mysterious matrix that represents the seed of creation, the universe in its unmanifest form. It symbolizes pure, undifferentiated consciousness and the point at which the microcosm and macrocosm meet. It is to this point that the meditator is drawn when gazing at or visualizing a yantra. Once reunited with the centre the meditator realizes his or her identity within universal consciousness.

In advanced practice, yogis construct yantras internally through visualization, often carried out in combination with other yogic practices such as the repetition of an appropriate mantra, without reference to any physical representation.

Visualizing a mandala or yantra

Although it is a more complex image and requires more advanced abilities, a mandala or yantra can be visualized in much the same way as the objects used for kasina meditations, described in the exercise on page 165, 'Visualizing the colour blue'.

Keeping your eyes and facial muscles relaxed, allow your gaze to rest on the central point of the mandala or yantra to begin with, then gradually extend outwards to the periphery and then slowly return to the centre. The corresponding mantras may be repeated while gazing at a yantra.

This magnificent mandala has been painstakingly constructed by Buddhist monks from Bhutan using coloured sand that has been poured into position grain by grain.

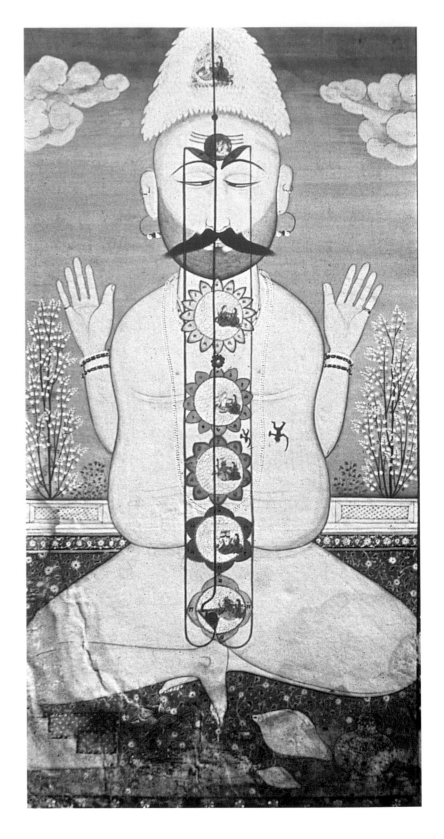

The principle chakras lie along a central channel located along the spinal axis, as illustrated in this colourful 18th century drawing from Himachal Pradesh, India.

Chakras

As described on pages 62–71, some forms of yoga – in particular hatha, kundalini and tantric yoga – are based on the concept of a 'subtle' body, a sort of ethereal version of the physical body that comprises a network of subtle channels and energy centres known as chakras. The main chakras lie along a central channel called the *sushumna*, which runs along the spine, and each is associated with a visual symbol, or yantra, and a bija or seed mantra, a symbolic sound representing potentiality. The central aim of these forms of yoga is to arouse the divine power known as the *kundalini*, which is said to lie dormant in the *muladhara* chakra at the base of the spine, and raise it up to the *sahasrara*, the centre at the crown of the head, at which point individual consciousness merges with divine consciousness and the yogi becomes enlightened.

Traditionally, the ascent of the kundalini is effected by meditating successively on each of the chakras, beginning with the lowest, visualizing the chakra in question while mentally repeating the seed mantra associated with it. As the kundalini rises, it pierces the energy centres, finally dissolving in the thousand-petalled centre at the crown of the head. Visualization may be accompanied by the exercise of various forms of breath control, gestures and muscular 'locks'. Complex meditation is best carried out under the supervision of a qualified teacher, but simpler forms of visualizing the chakras can be carried out using the method described above for visualizing a mandala or yantra, using the descriptions of the individual chakras on pages 64–65.

Alternatively you may like to try the meditation exercise opposite, which is adapted from an ancient book of yoga called the *Vijnana Bhairava*. Rather than passing through each chakra, in this meditation the kundalini is visualized as shooting forth directly from the base to the crown chakra.

The lightning-like ascent of the kundalini

Read the meditation instructions through completely once or twice before you begin. You may find it helpful to record them, but be sure to leave plenty of space between each instruction.

Sit comfortably in any cross-legged position, or on a chair if you prefer with your feet flat on the floor. Hold your back, head and neck erect yet relaxed. Tuck in your chin and place your hands in your lap or on your thighs. With the weight of your body centred over your sitting bones, feel these bones pressing down and your spine elongating, as though an invisible string were lifting you from the base of your spine through the crown of your head towards the ceiling. A cushion placed beneath you will raise your hips and help keep the back in an upright position, increasing the flow of meditative energy circulating through the body. Close or half-close your eyes and spend a few moments consciously relaxing your body. Scan it for any pockets of tension and relax with the help of your breath, breathing in energy, breathing out tension.

Now bring your awareness to the base of your spine and visualize the kundalini, the divine energy, arising from the muladhara chakra, scintillating like the rays of the sun and rising like a flash of lightning to the centre at the crown of the head. Meditate on the kundalini dissolving in the light of universal consciousness as it finishes its journey.

At the end of the session open your eyes slowly and sit quietly for a few moments, acknowledging your meditation and feeling the light of pure consciousness permeating your everyday awareness.

Variation: Meditate on the kundalini as a column of golden light rising up the spine, ascending from centre to centre and piercing each individual chakra, until it reaches the crown of the head and merges into the light of universal consciousness.

GURUS and TEACHERS

4

The supreme revelation of God appears in prophets and holy men. To venerate them is true veneration of God.   *I Ching*

The glory of the guru – the illumined being who can ignite the spark of spiritual energy within a seeker – has been extolled since time immemorial, particularly in the East. Of course, the guidance of an experienced teacher is an advantage in most endeavours, but despite superficial similarities and techniques, there is a deep gulf between meditating to relax a little and meditating as a way to spiritual enlightenment. The goals you want to achieve through meditation bring an energy of their own to the process, giving rise to different experiences and results. If you meditate mainly for the physical and emotional benefits, the guidance of any teacher you feel comfortable with, who has reasonable experience of meditation – or even the guidance offered in a book! – will enable you to establish a practice. If you practise meditation as part of a spiritual journey, then working with a genuine teacher who can inspire you, keep you from stumbling over the many obstacles that may lie ahead and get you back on track if you do, and help you understand any experiences that may arise, is of incalculable benefit. Such a teacher should be well travelled in the inner terrain and familiar with the territory, and at the very least several steps ahead of you.

Much more, however, is claimed for the *sadguru* or 'true teacher', whose mere touch, look, word or thought can initiate (see page 181), kick-starting a seeker's spiritual evolution through the transmission of power. This transmission activates the seeker's own latent inner energy and accelerates his or her progress along the path. Once this inner awakening has taken place, the practitioner is naturally drawn inward into meditative states. Teachers such as this have immense spiritual power and their mere presence can have the most extraordinary impact on the spiritual lives of their disciples. They are hard to find, however, and unfortunately there are plenty of self-styled gurus who will be more than happy to accept your money and adulation, but leave you no wiser except in some of the more unscrupulous ways of the world. All too often the relationship with a guru ends in disillusionment and heartbreak, though usually the warning signs become apparent in time for intelligent and sincere seekers to disentangle themselves before lasting damage is done.

When assessing a teacher it is advisable to bear in mind that appearances can be deceptive. The teachers that seem to have the most burning sincerity and faith can turn out to be the most dangerous, the most deluded. The teachers that behave in a predictable and conventional fashion, offering consistent teachings that are in line with scriptural authority, may nevertheless fail to kindle the spiritual flame within their students. Yet the 'crazy wisdom' teachers, unconcerned with convention, and often teaching in unpredictable and seemingly irrational ways, may succeed where others fail, propelling their students into different states of consciousness with their spiritual shock tactics. Rather than offering spiritual instruction and lifestyle guidelines, their method is to shatter the limitations of rational thought and cut through the illusion of a separate self.

Of those teachers with genuine spiritual gifts to offer, unfortunately many eventually become corrupted by the adulation of their devotees and the absolute power invested in them, and end up with reputations tarnished by accusations of sexual or financial misdemeanours. Mass devotion and attention combined with idealized concepts about how spiritual teachers should behave brings about their downfall. Impossible standards arc sct and then devotees feel let down when they are not achieved. One of the great fallacies amongst the devotees of some great spiritual leaders is that they are beyond normal human standards of behaviour. But even enlightened beings are also human beings, albeit those who perform a divine function. As members of the human race they have their personalities, likes and dislikes, and are fallible, just like anyone else. And eventually their bodies wither away and die, just like any others. This does not necessarily take away from their greatness, in the form of the spiritual power that flows through them and ignites the flame in others.

Since you will be investing a huge amount in any relationship with a spiritual teacher it pays to choose carefully. How, then, to find the teacher who is right for you?

Considered by many to be an enlightened master, Osho (1931–1990), formerly known as Bhagwan Shree Rajneesh, was a controversial teacher who taught an eclectic mix of Eastern mysticism and meditation, Western cathartic therapies and bodywork, and sexual freedom.

Beware of false prophets, which come to you in sheep's clothing, but inwardly they are ravening wolves.

Matthew 7:15

This 14th century fresco from a church in Padua, Italy, shows Christ demonstrating

his humility by washing the feet of his disciples at the Last Supper.

It is often said that when the seeker is ready the teacher appears. Some would add that we get the gurus we deserve, in which case working on being the right disciple may be a wiser option than going out looking for a teacher. A lot can be learnt from someone who may not be the teacher you ultimately end up with. In fact, most people on a spiritual path work with several teachers before they find their ultimate teacher, just as a budding virtuoso is likely to learn from a number of teachers before attending master classes with a maestro.

That said, often you just

Finding a genuine teacher

'know' when you find the teacher who is right for you. There's a sense of destiny. Even so, it is wise to be sceptical, even mistrustful, and keep your distance until you are convinced beyond doubt. The ultimate test of a teacher is your own inner experience, whether or not you grow spiritually in relationship with that teacher.

One's choice of teacher along the spiritual path is as important as one's choice of a life or marriage partner – and those who marry in haste repent at leisure, as the saying goes. A genuine teacher will enlighten and liberate you, not entrap you.

Warning signs

The true Guru will never humiliate you, nor will he estrange you from yourself. He will constantly bring you back to the fact of your inherent perfection and encourage you to seek within... The self-appointed Guru is more concerned with himself than his disciples.

Nisargadatta Maharaj, (1895–1986), spiritual leader

Not all teachers are quite as advanced spiritually as they would have you believe, but they may well be advanced con men. Detecting the warning signs is not quite as straightforward as it might at first seem, but the following rules of thumb, though not infallible, can help put you on your guard:

● Avoid any teacher who claims to be uniquely enlightened. Truth is the monopoly of no one.

● Avoid teachers who demand uncritical acceptance or absolute obedience, or who set tests of loyalty that may require you to violate your own code of behaviour.

● Be wary of teachers who cultivate dependency on the part of their students – for example, by creating an environment in which it is the norm to get the approval of the leader for important personal decisions, or by encouraging students to give up careers, relationships and so forth. A genuine teacher will liberate his or her students, not entrap them.

● Spiritual attainment is charismatic, but watch out for teachers who actively encourage the cult of personality (theirs!).

● Beware any forms of exploitation, the most common of which are sexual and financial (although there are subtler ways in which unscrupulous teachers can exploit their students). It is perfectly acceptable for teachers or spiritual organizations to ask for appropriate donations, but charging extortionate fees or encouraging students to make large donations they can ill afford – often by playing on their emotional insecurities – is not.

● Distrust teachers who do not practise what they preach.

● Distrust teachers who take themselves too seriously or lack a sense of humour.

You have to become your own
teacher and your own disciple.

Jiddu Krishnamurti, 20th century spiritual leader

Students and organisations

It is frequently the disciples rather than their teachers who
create – and run – the communities and organisations that
spring up around charismatic leaders. Although you cannot
assess a teacher just in terms of his or her students, observing
the effect the relationship with their teacher has on students,
and the culture that operates within such a group, can tell you
a great deal. Watch out for:

● Spiritual elitism: any group who claims that theirs is the
only 'Way', or that their particular philosophy represents the
ultimate truth.

● Denunciation of other religious or spiritual traditions and
teachers.

● An atmosphere of secrecy rather than openness. The
suppression of information, or its restriction to a tight inner
circle. Taboo subjects and a culture in which opinions cannot
be voiced, doubts cannot be aired and free-thinking is dis-
couraged.

● Intimidation, particularly of those within the group who do
not toe the party line or of those who have left.

● A hierarchical structure.

The inner teacher

*Going within means just listening to your own Guru. And
this Guru is your own Self. The real Guru will introduce
you to the Guru within and ask 'you' to keep quiet. This is
your own grace. It comes from within you. No one else
can give you this grace.*   Poonjaji, 20th century Indian guru

Whatever our expectations of a spiritual teacher may be, however close or rich our relationship with the external teacher,
and however wise he or she may be, ultimately we have to tap
into the wisdom that lies in our own hearts – the inner teacher. A true teacher points the way to this inner teacher and
awakens the spiritual process. The latter is called initiation.

Without *abhisheka* (initiation) our attempts to achieve spirituality will result in no more than a huge spiritual collection.   Chogyam Trungpa

Initiation

The inner teacher is already present within each one of us in the form of divine energy, or primal awareness, but this often remains dormant until awakened by an enlightened teacher. Initiation ignites the inner flame of spiritual knowledge, bringing teachings to life and setting in motion a spiritual process that will eventually lead to the supra-conscious state. It also creates an inner connection between the teacher and disciple, which is said to continue beyond the physical death of either one. Inner awakening becomes apparent in all aspects of one's life, but is particularly evident in meditation, which arises almost effortlessly.

Spiritual initiation is not a matter of taking vows or conducting secret ceremonies, though ritual may play a part in the proceedings. There are various ways in which inner awakening – also known as kundalini awakening – can take place, but the easiest and most effective method is said to be through the transmission of power from an enlightened or spiritually advanced teacher. This can literally be felt as a bolt of energy coursing through the body, empowering the initiate and often giving rise to a different state of consciousness. Although this experience may not last, the initiation is an irreversible process that jump-starts the seeker's inner evolution, unlocking the door to the inner realm and propelling him or her forward on the spiritual path. An illumined sage can initiate by his or her mere glance, word, touch or thought. Initiation can also take place when the teacher is not physically present, sometimes through dreams or visions, and through

spiritual instruction such as the giving of a mantra, a sacred sound or syllable, together with directions as to how to repeat it. Depending on the initiate's receptivity and level of development, he or she may instantly experience the bliss of the ultimate truth, though this is likely to be a temporary state, which can only be fully established by further spiritual work.

To receive spiritual transmission the student must be open, like the proverbial empty vessel ready to be filled. A Zen story tells of a master who received a visit from an eminent professor, who came to ask about Zen teachings. The Zen master picked up a teapot and began to fill the professor's bowl with tea. To the professor's astonishment and discomfort, once the bowl was filled to the rim the master kept on pouring, so the tea overflowed down the sides of the bowl. As he watched, the professor, unable to restrain himself, begged the master to stop pouring. 'Just as the bowl will hold no more,' replied the master, 'your mind contains too many opinions and preconceptions. To receive the teachings you must first become empty.'

Only when you have no thing in your mind and no mind in things are you vacant and spiritual, empty and marvellous.

Te-Shan

Kabir

Little is known about the early life of the great poet-saint Kabir, whose visionary poetry has inspired generations of Indians and, in translation, seekers of truth around the world. Many legends have grown up around his life, one of which tells how he became a disciple of the celebrated guru Ramananda.

In Ramananda Kabir recognized his destined guru, but as the son of a Muslim weaver, Kabir knew he would never be accepted by the Hindu guru as a disciple, so he devised a clever plan to receive the master's unwitting initiation. Knowing of Ramananda's custom of bathing in the holy waters of the Ganges early each morning, Kabir concealed himself on one of the steps leading down to the river and lay in wait for him. As Ramananda descended the steps, barefoot, he trod on the waiting Kabir, and called out, 'Ram, Ram,' the name of the Hindu deity he worshipped, in astonishment. In this way Kabir not only received the mantra of initiation from Ramananda, but was touched by the guru's feet, which are traditionally considered to be a spiritual power point, from which divine energy is transmitted. Ramananda went on his way, having inadvertently initiated the young Kabir, who in time became fully enlightened.

The story illustrates the primacy of the seeker's acceptance of a teacher over the acceptance of a disciple by the teacher. Kabir went on to become one of the greatest and most loved poets in the history of Indian mysticism, drawing equally from the symbolism of Hinduism and Islam. As he said of himself, he was 'at once the child of Allah and of Ram'.

O brother, my heart yearns for
   that true guru, who fills the cup
   of true love, and drinks of it
   himself, and offers it then to me.
He removes the veil from the eyes,
   and gives the true vision of
   Brahma (Supreme Reality):
He reveals the worlds in Him,
   and makes me to hear the
   unstruck music:
He shows joy and sorrow to be one:
He fills all utterance with love.

Songs of Kabir, Kabir

Sandals symbolically represent the guru and the bestowing of divine grace, which is why they are sometimes installed in places of meditation, often decorated with flowers, red kumkum powder and other offerings.

Gurus of the Siddha yoga lineage

Swami Muktananda (1908–82) was a Siddha guru of legendary power who awakened the inner meditative energy of thousands of seekers around the world through *shaktipat*, a form of initiation involving the transmission of a powerful current of spiritual energy into the disciple.

His own search for spiritual fulfilment began at a young age, with the practice of various forms of yoga and meditation, but Muktananda often claimed that his spiritual journey did not begin in earnest until many years later, when he received shaktipat from his own guru, Bhagawan Nityananda, and began to follow the Siddha path. Intense spiritual practices followed his inner awakening and nine years later he became fully enlightened and established an ashram in Ganeshpuri, in the Indian state of Maharashtra. In the 1970s Muktananda brought the teachings of Siddha Yoga to the West and set up a worldwide organization of ashrams and meditation centres, which now flourish under the leadership of Swami Chidvilasanada (see opposite).

Swami Muktananda was a charismatic and humorous leader with a larger-than-life character, but his final years were clouded by controversy, with accusations of questionable Tantric practices involving intimate relationships with some female disciples. Despite moral differences, however, few who received initiation from him, or who experienced the palpable power of his presence, would deny the transforming effect he had on their spiritual development, and the deepened sense of self-awareness that resulted from it.

Meditate on your own Self. God dwells within you as you.   Swami Muktananda

Swami Chidvilasananda, known affectionately to her devotees as 'Gurumayi', is the glamorous and charismatic spiritual heir of Swami Muktananda. Although the Siddha Yoga lineage was originally handed down to her jointly with her brother, Swami Nityananda, after three years he stepped down, having admitted to breaking his vows of celibacy.

Controversy surrounds the manner of Nityananda's departure and Gurumayi's role in it, but without doubt she has emerged as the undisputed successor to the substantial and worldwide network of ashrams and meditation centres established by Muktananda. Although she makes periodic visits to India, Gurumayi is based in South Fallsburg, in the Catskill Mountains of New York, where she attracts a fashionable following including several A-list celebrities. Gurumayi is a thoroughly modern spiritual leader who carries on the work of her guru, bestowing shaktipat initiation and transmitting the experience of Siddha Yoga, both by traditional means, such as chanting and meditation, and through music, art, drama and storytelling.

Swami Nityananda Initiated as a monk in 1980, at the age of eighteen, by Swami Muktananda, Swami Nityananda was installed as his joint successor to the Siddha Yoga lineage in 1982. Following his resignation three years later, in 1987 Swami Nityananda founded a spiritual community called Shanti Mandir as a vehicle for continuing the spiritual work of his guru. In 1995 he was ordained as a Mahamandaleshwar, a significant spiritual honour which he is the youngest person in history ever to have received.

Nityananda is a gentle and unassuming leader in the shaktipat tradition, whose teachings spring from the philosophy of Vedanta. His followers participate in the traditional practices of chanting, meditation, study, the offering of service and the performance of sacred rituals.

When you meditate, the silence of the senses illumines the presence of God within.   Gurumayi Chidvilasananda

Only when we make our heart a temple of peace can the meaning and purpose of our existence become known.   Swami Nityananda

Georgei Ivanovich Gurdjieff and the Work

G.I. Gurdjieff (c. 1866–1949) was born of a Greek father and an Armenian mother in a region of Russian Armenia where Eastern and Western cultures mingled and sometimes clashed, an influence that is apparent in his later writings. Considered by some to be the greatest mystical teacher of all time, and by others as a fraud, his teachings are still enormously influential. Gurdjieff believed that along with the awakening of consciousness, the direct awareness of who and what we really are, came the awakened conscience, the development of inner moral power.

From an early age Gurdjieff travelled throughout Central Asia and the Middle East, where he encountered various esoteric teachings, becoming especially influenced by Sufism and Tibetan Buddhism. Gurdjieff believed that man is asleep, an automaton responding mechanically to unconscious tendencies and external events. To become truly human he needs to evolve spiritually through inner work. The spiritual path Gurdjieff developed is called the Fourth Way, to distinguish it from the three classical paths of the fakir, the monk and the yogi. Today it is more commonly known as the Work, a term popularized by P.D. Ouspensky, one of Gurdjieff's best-known pupils (see opposite). The foundations of this path include various activities from hard physical labour and psychological exercises, to sacred dance movements based on those of the Sufi dervish dances, to meditation. Music and other art forms were also instrumental in his teaching. Gurdjieff believed that all arts serve a sacred purpose as

repositories of higher knowledge, and viewed ancient Eastern art forms – such as the mandalas of Tibetan Buddhism – as maps of consciousness that could be read like a book.

Like all great spiritual teachers, however, Gurdjieff's aim was to awaken rather than indoctrinate, and this included the use of spiritual 'shock' tactics. At the Prieuré, the community he established in Fontainebleau, near Paris, he used unpredictable and unconventional methods to this purpose. For example, students would be awoken at all hours to work or participate in group activities. Or, after living on an austere and frugal diet for weeks, they would be summoned to join Gurdjieff in bacchanalian feasting and drinking sessions. This brought about a certain amount of notoriety, which was exacerbated when the dying author Katherine Mansfield was accepted into the community.

Besides Katherine Mansfield, Gurdjieff attracted numerous artists and intellectuals, whose work flowered under the inner transformation they experienced around him. His teachings were carried on after his death through the work of students such as Ouspensky, A.R. Orage, the editor of the British journal *The New Age*, and Maurice Nichol, a pioneering English psychologist who also worked with C.J. Jung. Today the teachings continue to be transmitted orally in organized groups through second and third generation pupils all over the world.

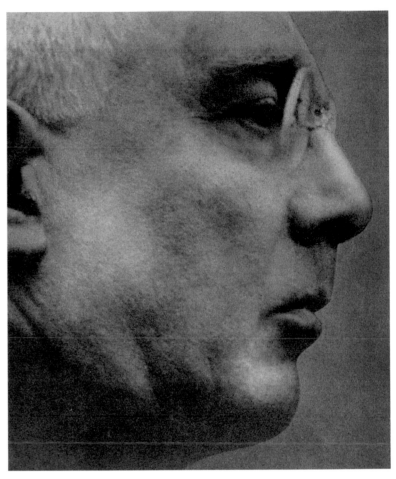

Know that you must seek the Way.
The Way does not seek you out!   Gurdjieff

Pyotr Demianovitch Ouspensky

The philosopher P.D. Ouspensky (1878–1949) was born of an artistic and intellectual Russian family. He became one of Gurdjieff's most prominent students, studying with him intensively for a few years, and going on to produce the influential *In Search of the Miraculous*, the best account of Gurdjieff's teachings. Although he later broke with Gurdjieff, he nevertheless continued to be a leading exponent of the teachings through his own study groups.

His Holiness the Dalai Lama

The Dalai Lama, meaning 'ocean of wisdom', is the spiritual and secular leader of the Tibetan people, who usually refer to His Holiness as Kundun, 'the Presence'. This epithet denotes spiritual power and anyone who has had the good fortune to attend the talks or simply be in the presence of the much-loved and revered current Dalai Lama, Tenzin Gyatso, can attest to this. Tenzin Gyatso, born in 1935, is the fourteenth of a succession of incarnations of the Dalai Lama, but since 1960 has lived in exile in Dharamsala, India, following the Chinese seizure of Tibet.

From his base in India, the Dalai Lama has continued to draw attention to the plight of his people, travelling world-wide to spread his message. In doing so he has greatly increased awareness and the popularity of Tibetan Buddhism. Yet along with spiritual figures of the stature of Mahatma Gandhi and Mother Teresa, the Dalai Lama has transcended the barriers of religion, reaching out beyond his own tradition of Buddhism, and teaching a way of spirituality that finds a universal audience.

Awarded the Nobel peace prize in 1989, the Dalai Lama is a leading proponent of human rights and world peace. He is also a prolific author and has written extensively on Tibetan Buddhism. He recommends meditation, whether simple methods of concentration or the complex techniques of Tibetan Buddhism, as a spiritual practice and as a way to inner peace and lasting happiness.

If we can realize and meditate on ultimate truth, it will cleanse our impurities of mind and thus eradicate the sense of discrimination.   Dalai Lama

Index

Author's acknowledgments

Writing *The Spirit of Meditation* has reinvigorated my own practice and offered a wonderful opportunity to learn more about other traditions of meditation. Warm thanks to Camilla Stoddart for proposing I write it, and for her sensitivity and help in shaping the text. I am also grateful to all at Cassell Illustrated who have helped create such a magnificent book, especially Robin Douglas-Withers for her boundless patience, good humour and observant editorial attention, and Gabrielle Mander for the personal interest she has taken. Huge thanks also to Joanna Burton for demonstrating yoga and meditation positions with such poise and serenity; Terry Benson for his beautiful photos; Ros Bell for entrusting to me her Zen brush painting by Shifu Nagaboshi Tomio, and to both of them for generously giving permission for its inclusion in the book; Jane Hindley, Soni Veliz and David Bomford for their vision and marvellous illustration suggestions; Simon Wilder for a strong design; Nicholas Wilks for contributing to my understanding of different religious traditions; Ann Hunt for her perceptive comments on the text and helpful suggestions; and Fern Clarke for her splendid contribution to the section on Christianity.

I could not have written the book without the help of countless individuals who have given their time so generously and shared their knowledge and enthusiasm for meditation with me. Special thanks to Donny, wherever you are, for introducing me to meditation in the first place. Fond thanks also to Marinella Franks for coming with me to ashrams, Sufi communities and meditation centres, and of course for *that* copy of *Harpers Bazaar*. Writing about gurus, teachers and spiritual organisations has helped me resolve some of my own issues and I would particularly like to thank Sally Kempton for her insights, and the clarity of her vision and teachings on meditation. I am also profoundly grateful to the other exceptional yoga and meditation teachers I have been privileged to know and learn from, especially Baba Muktananda, whose ability to ignite the fire of meditation and keep it aflame was legendary, and B.K.S. Iyengar, whose consummate knowledge of yoga and rare gift for teaching have brought international acclaim. Additional and heartfelt thanks to Mr Iyengar for his generous foreword.

Finally, appreciative thanks to my husband, the publisher Nicholas Brealey, for his keen eye, wise advice and wicked sense of humour; and to both Nick and Sam for their amazing tolerance.

Picture credits

The publishers would like to thank the following for permission to reproduce their material. Every care has been taken to trace copyright holders. However, if we have omitted anyone we apologise and shall, if informed, make corrections in any future editions.

AKG, London/Erich Lessing 111 /Robert O'Dea 81; **Bridgeman Art Library, London**/Mark Rothko 'Red' © 1998 Kate Rothko Prizel&Christopher Rothko/DACS 2004 121 /Scrovegni Chapel, Padua 176 /Lauros/Giraudon 141 /National Museum of Karachi, Karachi Pakistan 48 /Constantin Brancusi 'Sleeping Muse' 111/c.1971 © ADAGP, Paris and DACS, London 2004 118 /Roger-Viollet, Paris 98-99 /National Museum of Scotland 83, 84 /Untitled ("Winged Curve") (1966) Bridget Riley © the artist 16; **Corbis UK Ltd** 74, 77, 142 /Archivo Iconografico S.A 103 /Burstein Collection 92 /Charles & Josette Lenars 78 /Sheldan Collins 148 /Michael Freeman 126, 155 /Arvind Garg 55

/Lindsey Hebberd 71 /Henry Diltz 19 /Jeremy Horner 169 /Gauvriel Jecan 137 /Mark A. Johnson 24 /Charles & Josette Lenars 146 /Chris Lisle 28-29, 90-91 /Francis G. Mayer 113 /Micael Pole 116-117 /David Samuel Robbins 69 /Phil Schermeister 180 /Janez Skok 50 /Gregor Schmidt 150 /Keren Su 42 /Adam Woolfitt 152; **Eye Ubiquitous**/The Hutchison Library/Felix Greene 97 /Jeremy Horner 67; **Getty Images**/Brian Bailey 14-15 /Rosemary Calvert 37 /John Chapple 33 /Jody Dole 158 /Michael Dunning 163 /Ed Freeman 2 /Grant Faint 47 /Lena Leon 156 /Matthew Naythons 175 /Photodisc Red 125 /Steve Satushek 34 /Karen Su 129 /Simon Watson 138; **Lisson Gallery**/ Anish Kapoor 'At the Hub of Things' 1987 (fiberglass and pigment) Collection Hirshhorn Museum and Sculpture Garden, Washington DC, Susan Ormeord 164; **Mary Evans Picture Library** 187 left, 187 right; **Octopus Publishing Group Ltd**/Terry Benson 23, 56, 57, 58-59, 59 top, 60-61, 130, 132, 133 left, 133 right, 134, 135, 183; **Oxford Scientific Films** 122; **Paragon Press**/Shirazeh Houshiary, 'Round Dance' colour etching) 1992,Scottish National Gallery of Modern Art 100; **The Picture Desk Ltd.**/The Art Archive/Biblioteca Nacional Lisbon/Dagli Orti 104 /Bodleian Library, Oxford 107; **www.pictorialpress.com** 20; **Pictures Colour Library**/Intervision Ltd 108; **Ramamani Iyengar Memorial Yoga Institute** 7; **Ros Bell**/Shifu Nagaboshi Tomio 86; **Thames & Hudson Ltd**/ Ajit Mookerjee Collection. From 'Tantra:The Cult of Ecstasy' by Phillip Rawson 62, 170, /Ajit Mookerjee Collection. From 'The Art of Tantra' by Philip Rawson 167 /Ajit Mookerjee Collection. From 'Yoga Art' by Ajit Mookerjee 72–3; **Tibet Images**/ Shane Rozzario 189; **TopFoto**/The British Museum 89; **Werner Forman Archive** 30;

Other Permissions

p. 20 Lyrics from 'Within You Without You' © 1967 Northern Songs Limited – Sony/ATV Music Publishing Limited

Publisher's acknowledgments

Cassell Illustrated would like to thank Rebecca Mercer for the six hand-painted chakra mandalas on page 64, which are reprinted from Donald Butler's *Ten-Minute Yoga* with the author's kind permission, and Ghost, Red Hot and Bodas for the clothing worn on pages 23, 56–61, 130 and 132–135 (www.ghost.co.uk, www.redhotfashions.co.uk and www.bodas.co.uk).

Cassell Illustrated would also like to acknowledge the following sources: p. 18 'The Marriage of Heaven and Hell' and p. 152 'Auguries of Innocence' from *The Poems of William Blake*, Routledge & Kegan Paul, 1905; p. 25 'Burnt Norton' from *Four Quartets*, T.S. Eliot, Faber and Faber, 1944; p.30 'Choruses from 'The Rock' ' from *The Waste Land and Other Poems*, T.S. Eliot, Faber and Faber, 1940; 'p. 76 Paracelsus' by Robert Browning from *The Oxford Book of English Mystical Verse*, Clarendon Press, 1917; p. 92–99 *Te-Tao Ching* transl. by Robert G. Henricks, The Bodley Head Ltd., 1989 and *The Tao Te Ching by Lao Tzu*, transl. by Stephen Mitchell, Macmillan, 1989; p. 24, 40, 42, 142, 182 *Songs of Kabir*, transl. by Rabindranath Tagore, Samuel Weiser Inc, 1915; p. 103 'The Beloved' by Jalalludin Rumi from *The Way of the Sufi*, Idries Shah, Penguin, 1974; p. 144 'Ulysses' and p. 150 'The Ancient Sage', from *Alfred, Lord Tennyson* (selected poems), Penguin, 1991; p. 149 Tennyson's letter to Mr B.P. Blood from *Cosmic Consciousness* by R.M. Bucke, Dutton & Co, 1923, first published in 1901, p. 174 The I Ching, Routledge & Kegan Paul, 1951;